"Ginger reminds us that before the fairy tale we and dream job comes God. She will challenge for you with passion and priority. Let Ginger's words and experience sink deep into your heart and mind. You will come out new."

—Carey C. Bailey,
Author of *Cravings: Desiring God in the Midst of Motherhood*

"I think this is the most practical and wisdom-filled book on purity and dating that I've read in a while (if ever). For me, it easily lined out what Scripture says about the purity of our hearts and bodies, as well as going above and beyond the "don't do it!" It answered lots of questions that I know my girls struggle with and will encourage them to think about how they are currently treating their own hearts."

—Lauren Carnathan,
Youth Minister

"Ginger is authentic and full of passion to see every girl walking in their true identity in Christ and all the fullness God has for them. She did a great job of incorporating her humor, the truth of God's Word and personal stories into a wonderful and interactive book. Girls of all ages will be able to relate to her struggles, questions and experiences. I look forward to using her book as a resource when mentoring high school girls and would definitely recommend it to all my friends!"

—Elise Smith,
Wife, Mom, Disciple Maker and Teacher

"I wish I had read this book when I was in high school, or even junior high! Just the same, it has proven to be useful for a young lady, such as myself, in college. *Forget the Corsage* is one of those books you'll always have somewhere nearby, no matter what season of life you find yourself in. Each page is filled with so much truth that it's hard not to refer back to it every once in a while."

—Elizabeth Andronic,
College Freshman

"Ginger starts each chapter with a topic girls my age often worry about. She digs into her own past (and lets us go with her on numerous occasions) to provide a real-life situation that instantly makes things more personal and therefore easier to apply to our lives. Attacking the problem head-on, she breaks it down into its most basic parts and provides undeniably clear explanations for anything we might find confusing, all the while filling the book to the brim with an abundance of sound Scripture. Beautifully written and extremely impactful, this book should be in the hands of girls everywhere."

—Lindsay Mostrom,
High School Junior

Forget the Corsage

Life Starts Now

GINGER CIMINELLO

WESTBOW
PRESS
A DIVISION OF THOMAS NELSON

WestBow Press books may be ordered through booksellers or by contacting:

WestBow Press
A Division of Thomas Nelson
1663 Liberty Drive
Bloomington, IN 47403
www.westbowpress.com
1-(866) 928-1240

Author photo provided by Andrea Alley Photography.

All Scripture quotations, unless otherwise indicated, are taken from The Holy Bible, New International Version, NIV ®, NIV® Copyright © 1973, 1978, 1984, 2011 by Biblica, Inc.™ Used by permission. All rights reserved worldwide.

Scripture quotations marked GW are taken from God's Word Translation ®, © 1995 God's Word to the Nations. Used by permission of Baker Publishing Group.

Scripture quotations marked NLT are taken from the Holy Bible, New Living Translation© 1996, 2004, 2007 by Tyndale House Foundation. Used by permission of Tyndale House Publishers, Inc., Carol Stream, Illinois, 60188. All rights reserved.

Scripture quotations marked NKJV are taken from the New King James Version®. Copyright © 1982 by Thomas Nelson, Inc. Used by permission. All rights reserved.

Scripture quotations marked MSG are taken from The Message. Copyright © 1993, 1994, 1995, 1996, 2000, 2001, 2002. Used by permission of NavPress Publishing Group.

ISBN: 978-1-4908-0255-8 (sc)
ISBN: 978-1-4908-0256-5 (hc)
ISBN: 978-1-4908-0254-1 (e)

Library of Congress Control Number: 2013912979

Printed in the United States of America.

WestBow Press rev. date: 08/20/2013

For Amy,
who reminds me that it's never too cold, too
hot, too early, or too late to dance.

And for David,
who was perfectly formed for my heart.

Contents

Acknowledgments

It is with the deepest gratitude and appreciation that I say thanks to the many names listed below. I could fill an additional book with reasons why you have made this dream a reality. Your interest, prayers, concerns, and shared joys have meant everything to me during this process. I am indebted to you. Thank you always.

My one and only David, your support made this happen. Your sacrifice and love push me to be the woman God designed me to be. Thank you for helping me see and remember when fear gets in the way.

My baby girl, you are on each and every page. I hope and pray that you will know the source of life and that your light will shine brightly for the Lord. I cannot wait to be your cheerleader.

Mom and Dad, my cheerleaders, through your examples of faith you have encouraged and challenged me more than you will ever know. I am proud to be your daughter.

My go-to for everything is Val, whose opinions I trust and value. You are so much more than my sister. You are my editor, coach, confidante, and friend. Blue scales!

My source of laughter is Clayboy, who makes me smile. Your heart is big and your capacity for love is so great. I cannot wait to see how your story unfolds.

I thank my tireless editors, Dalynda, Renea, and Jordan, for shaping my writing into something readable! I appreciate every note, comma, and piece of advice. Thank you for your genuine interest in this manuscript. Thank you more importantly for your friendship!

My faithful readers Carey, Elise, Lauren, Elizabeth, Lindsay, and Suzie, your thoughts, wisdom, and encouragement were such a blessing to me. This book is better because of you.

My consistent encouragers Grandma Ann, Grandpa Joe, Grandma Doris, Grandpa Glenn, Mike and Nancy, Ross and Lauren, Erin, Virginia, Shannon, Kathy, the Bates family, Kacie, Becca, Megan, Sarah, and Annie, thank you for being you, for asking how this whole process was going, and then for asking again.

My inspiring teachers Carrie and Craig, Lynelle, Mandy, Jeanene, Donna, Joyous, Kevin, Matt, Chris, Scott, and Karrie, your words have influenced my life and the way I love the Lord. Thank you for your wisdom, your time, and your heart that you share so readily with those who sit at your feet. You will likely find yourselves quoted in these pages.

My initiators Ashleigh and Chris both said, "If you ever write a book, I will buy it." I salute you and reply, "Prove it!" Thanks for the kick in the pants.

And lastly, my heavenly Father, this is for You. Thank you for bringing me into Your story.

Introduction

When my cousin Amy entered the word, she filled all of our lives with joy. Born with a large hole in her heart and Down syndrome, she had to undergo many procedures in the first years of her life. As she grew older and healthier, Amy developed a quick wit and a wonderful sense of humor. Her quotes have stopped my entire family in its tracks and provided much-needed laughter. She is now in her early twenties, but I can still picture her as the toddler who wowed us with her ability to do splits and keep us dancing. Whether giving sold-out concert performances in the backyard or fiercely protective hugs, Amy stands out as a vibrant member of our huge family.

Once Amy hit twelve years old, she became concerned about the dating and relationship status of each of her cousins. I vividly remember having a brief heart-to-heart with her concerning my own relationships.

"Ginger," she began, "do you have a boyfriend?"

"No, Amy. No boyfriend," I quickly replied.

She tried again. "Ginger, how old are you?"

"I'm eighteen."

"Do you have a boyfriend?"

"Nope. No boyfriend."

"You're eighteen. You have a boyfriend."

Thinking I'd found a loophole, I countered, "You're right, Amy. Jesus is my boyfriend!"

Amy spun around, looked me squarely in the eyes, and asked accusingly, "Do you think I'm stupid?"

In that one moment, Amy spoke loudly and distinctly for her generation and for our culture. The truth is that most girls are expected to date, go to college, land a high-paying job, become engaged, get married, get pregnant, and *then* live happily ever after. The expectation for *most* American young women is to have it all: an elite education, a powerful career, and a love story that rivals Disney.

My concern is not desire in and of itself. I believe our hearts are wired to want and desire all kinds of good things! My concern comes with our tendency—specifically as girls—to idolize relationships with guys. Amy's interrogation was just the beginning.

Once I reached high school, I noticed that I could rarely finish a conversation without being asked, "Are you dating anyone?" Sometimes, I could handle that question, but other times, it would leave me in a state of panic because usually *I didn't have that someone.*

In fact, I lived through my entire high school journey in anticipation of my senior prom. I had the dress, the heels, and the up-do, but I did not have the date. At the last minute, I recruited a friend to accompany me. He was to pick me up at the house, escort me to dinner, and drive me to the dance. And of course, he was supposed to bring me a corsage. Instead, my date arrived to the dance after ten o'clock, rushing in to find me standing at the bottom of the escalator that had already delivered my entire senior class to their "night to remember." I had waited by myself for over an hour because I was convinced that I couldn't enter the dance until I had my date and my corsage. I danced to only three songs that night and spent most of my prom thinking, *No one will ever want me. My life is never going to start.*

Since that time, God has challenged me with my own words. That night, I believed two lies that many of us are prone to believe.

1. I am unwanted and undesired.

2. My life hasn't started yet and will only begin when I find *the one.*

If I truly am a daughter of the King of Kings, then I know the response to my own lament. Not only does God want me, but He has also given me an abundant and exciting life right from the start. His love provides the courage to live adventurously, regardless of my dating or marital status.

The Bible, God's love letter to us, reminds us that our desires are important to God. In fact, Psalm 37:4 says, "Delight yourself in the Lord and He will give you the desires of your heart." My desires encompass everything from my food preferences and clothing choices to the deepest wants and dreams for my life. This verse in Psalms tells me I will receive my desires, if I simply delight myself in the Lord. But what happens when you are twenty-seven, single, delighting yourself in the Lord, and still finding your desires out of reach? That's the real-life story I found myself living. The Lord has since taken me on a journey through His Word and through my past to discover a future that is secure in Him.

I wrote this book for every young woman who believes that life is on hold until she measures up to standards set by this world. My desire is to see *all* women come to be known by their identity in Jesus, including their God-given passions, rather than their dating status, career obligations, or how they compare to other women. You may be a daughter, a friend, a cousin, or a girlfriend, but your most important identity lies in who God has made you to be: His daughter. If you are seeking hope and purpose in your heavenly Father, then this book is *just* for you.

> "And this is my prayer: that your love may abound more and more in knowledge and depth of insight, so that you may be able to discern what is best and may be pure and blameless until the day of Christ."
> *Philippians 1:9–10*

CHAPTER 1

Forget the Corsage

… You know with all your heart and soul that not one of all
the good promises the Lord your God gave you has failed.
Every promise has been fulfilled; not one has failed.
Joshua 23:14–15

Dear Eighteen-Year-Old Ginger,

I know everyone else has been asked to the prom. I know that the guy
you were hoping would ask you has asked your friend. I know how
crummy this feels, but I want you to go ahead and ask one of your guy
friends. Even though he isn't going to show up until ten o'clock, it's going
to be okay. But *do not* wait for him to arrive. Do not stand outside your
senior prom waiting to go in for over an hour. Have fun. It's okay. A
date isn't a requirement to enjoy the dance or, for that matter, anything
else this life has to offer. Go and get your groove on.

Love,
Today's Ginger

Happily Ever After

> "Be merciful to me, O God, for men hotly pursue
> me; all day long they press their attack."
> *Psalm 56:1*

The senior year of high school is supposed to be the pinnacle of your secondary educational experience. It is the year of awards, SAT testing, parties, college preparation, homecoming ... The list could fill this book. But the zenith, the point outside of graduation that you spend your entire high school experience awaiting, is prom. Senior prom.

It was February of my senior year, two months before the big dance. I wasn't dating anyone, and my crush of three years just happened to be dating one of my friends. Perfect.

People were starting to pair off, and I still didn't have a date. So I did what I needed to do. I asked someone to be my date. I invited an energetic friend from my theater class. I figured if I couldn't go with a romantic lead, I would at least go with an amazing dancer.

My date and I determined to join a huge group of our friends—a group that happened to include my crush, Jay. (That wasn't going to be awkward, right?) The morning of the big day rolled around, and I heard from my date, Brian, that he had advanced in a speech and debate tournament and wouldn't be able to pick me up from the house. Not a problem. I placed his boutonniere in an orange Igloo lunchbox and had my mom drive me to the local country club for photos with the rest of the group.

It turned out my date did so well at the speech and debate tournament that he wasn't able to meet us for photos. So I sucked it up and lined up with the other girls for a photo. Of course, I was the only one not wearing a corsage, but at that moment, I wasn't going to be picky. A friend of mine offered to let me ride with her to the restaurant. Her boyfriend drove, and I sat in the backseat with my orange lunchbox.

We arrived at the restaurant, and it was quickly apparent that my date was not going to be joining us. I found my seat at the table and somehow ended up across from Jay and his date, Taylor. We ate. We conversed. I made it through.

I don't remember what I had for dinner, but I do remember the maître d' coming up to our table and asking if there was someone named Ginger in our party. I followed this guy through the restaurant, and he directed me to the telephone in a broom closet. I kid you not. I half-expected to run into Harry Potter as I picked up the phone.

My date's mother was calling—crying—and wanted me to know my date had advanced to the finals and was eligible for scholarships. He would be meeting me at the dance, and she would pay for dinner. It was difficult enough knowing my date wasn't going to make it, but it was even worse watching all the high school romances budding around me. I sucked it up and got back in the car with the happy couple and my orange lunchbox, and we headed downtown to Union Station.

Prom was a sweet setup. The school had rented a huge building with multiple rooms, and just about the entire graduating class of over one thousand seniors attended. We arrived, and I still had no date. The first thing I noticed upon entering was that the actual prom was still an escalator ride away. Looking up to the second floor, I spied silver streamers, dramatic fog, and a huge banner announcing that this was to be "A Night to Remember!" With the music bumping, my friends looked at me and I promptly waved them up the escalator to get their "happily ever after" on. At that point, it was 9:00 p.m. and prom ended at midnight. As I waited for my date, I became the official Walmart greeter for the dance. I'm pretty sure all 1,137 members of my senior class came late to prom that year, and I waved to and welcomed each one.

My date showed up around 10 p.m. He was apologetic and as energetic as ever as he hurried to the restroom to change into his tuxedo. By 10:30, we were finally taking the elevator up to the dance, although he had failed to retrieve my corsage, and his boutonniere still rested safely in the orange lunchbox in my friend's Taurus. We arrived at the top of the escalator where I took a deep breath, closed my eyes, and then walked through the streamers to what I hoped would be a magical land where my dreams would come true.

I was not disappointed by the decorations. They looked amazing: three different rooms for dancing, a line for photos, and an enormous buffet spread.

I started walking toward the biggest dance floor when my date let me know he had yet to eat anything. That's when my smile began to wear thin. I sent him off to the food while I headed outside to the balcony to get some air. The skyline of downtown Dallas was absolutely gorgeous. There were plenty of couples that had come to gaze at the view but had *somehow* found themselves making out instead. As I walked to the edge of the balcony, hurt and anxiety began to set in as I succumbed to the realization that *no one would ever want me.* Fearful words filled my head. *I'm always going to be this girl—the funny one. The one everyone wants to be friends with but not actually date. When it comes down to it, guys always ask someone else. I will always be the one waiting for my someone. I'll always be waiting for life to start.*

I danced a total of three dances at my senior prom, and only one was with my date. I never received my corsage. I did not end up marrying anyone who attended. That night, I was waiting for something. I was waiting for a date who would bring me my corsage and lead me up to the dance. For whatever reason—fear, the desire for approval, a lack of self-confidence—I desperately believed that I needed the date to take the escalator up to the dance.

Life Starts Now

I didn't miss out on my senior prom because the guy I liked didn't ask me. The experience does not go down in infamy because of a tardy dance partner. I missed out on enjoying the dance because I presupposed that I had to meet certain requirements to take the escalator.

Even as I graduated from high school and then attended college, I kept wondering when my life was really going to start. It's tempting to believe that life begins when we leave home for the first time. What I didn't realize was that my hopes and fears were actually keeping me frozen at the starting block. I, like so many others, had come to believe that meaningful living would be found sometime in my future.

"My ministry will begin when I graduate from college."

"My life will begin when I get married."

"My purpose will set in once I'm raising children."

I now believe many of us are stuck waiting for life to begin, if only someone would take our hand or give us a corsage. But life does not begin with a diploma, a career, or a date. The truth is that life started the moment we determined to follow Jesus and surrendered our lives to Him. We are waiting for something that has already been given: life to the full.

> "The thief comes only to steal and kill and destroy; I have come that they may have life, and have it to the full."
> *John 10:10*

Jesus, the son of the living God, said those words to a crowd full of living, breathing people. I'm sure they were puzzled at His strong words. Why would they possibly need more life?

I firmly believe that God is the creator of the world and all that is in it. The Bible shows God being actively involved in each moment of the creation. In the first few chapters of Genesis, we read about how God spoke the universe, the world, and even the garden of Eden into being. God created something out of nothing. One simple "Let there be light," and instantly light was made. He called forth the sun, moon, stars, oceans, land, plants, animals, and eventually humans. He looked at all He had made and declared it *good*. Once Adam and Eve were in the picture, He proclaimed His masterpiece to be *very good*.

When God created the world, His design was that His beloved creation might live in peace. *Shalom.* Have you ever heard that word before? It is a Hebrew greeting spoken by Jews around the world. According to *Strong's Concordance*, shalom means "completeness, wholeness, health, peace, welfare, safety soundness, tranquility, prosperity, perfectness, fullness, rest, harmony, the absence of agitation or discord. Shalom comes from the root verb shalom meaning to be complete, perfect, and full." [1]

In the very beginning, the relationship between God and man was at peace—complete, perfect, and whole. Can you imagine what that must have been like? Imagine your life without pain or hardship. Imagine never fearing the opinions of others or worrying about your body. Imagine having a perfect relationship with God without guilt or shame. Can you picture being fully at peace?

When I visualize being perfectly at peace, I think about floating in a swimming pool while the sunlight breaks through my closed eyes. I picture lying in a hammock while drifting in and out of sleep as the palm trees rustle. I remember staring up at the sky as I lay on a hot tennis court at dusk and watching shooting stars dance across the sky. Or I recall Christmas morning with family when there's a fire and the smell of baking cinnamon. What a full and joyful feeling. Those moments, however wonderful, are so brief compared to the worry and comparison I dwell upon each day. Something just isn't, well, perfect. Shalom has been damaged.

From the start, God had given Adam and Eve the option to eat from *any* tree in the garden, except one. The temptation proved too powerful as Satan appeared with his form of encouragement, telling Eve that she would not die from eating of the Tree of Knowledge of Good and Evil but that she would instead be like God. Eve ate, gave the fruit to Adam, and shalom was instantly disturbed. Since that time, our sin has continued to disrupt the peace that creation was designed to contain. This world and our relationships are broken. And when Jesus said that He had come to bring life, He was making a bold statement.

Left on our own, our relationship with God will remain broken. Shalom has been disrupted and we have been separated from His presence. Our sins, hardened hearts, and mistakes make sure of that. Satan and sin offer destruction and death, but Jesus offers life. Yet while we were powerless to fix our fallen way, Jesus came to give us a way back to shalom.

> "For the wages of sin is death, but the gift of God is
> eternal life through Jesus Christ our Lord."
> *Romans 6:23*

Jesus came to take our punishment and to pay the fee our sin demanded. The blameless Son of God lived a perfect life on this earth and then died a criminal's death upon a cross. He took our place. His death brought us life. And apart from Jesus, there is no life. In fact, 1 John 5:12 declares that without Jesus, we have no life.

"Whoever has the Son has life; whoever does not
have the Son of God does not have life."
1 John 5:12

Without Jesus, we can exist in this world, but we will not know the
full extent of shalom with our heavenly Father. If we do not know
Jesus, we will not know life to the full.

I can claim to know a lot of people, but in all honesty, I probably know
only a handful really well. When I ask you, "Do you know Jesus?" I
really want to know if you have found real, meaningful life in Him.
A majority of the population would say they know who Jesus is. They
acknowledge His existence and might even agree He was the Son of
God. But the Bible says, "Even the demons believe that and shudder"
(James 2:19b). So just believing that Jesus really walked the earth isn't
the same as really knowing Him.

I know my UPS deliveryman's name, but that's the extent of my
knowledge. Kevin is always friendly and waits patiently for me to
sign my name and collect my package. I know that he hurries off with
a smile after I've said, "Thank you!" Knowing Kevin hasn't really
changed me in any way. I do not make decisions based on his words
or life. Sometimes, our relationship with Jesus is just that. We might
be on a first-name basis, but knowing His name has made little or no
impact on our lives. But He never intended it to be that way. We were
designed for relationship with the one who loved and made us.

Life starts with knowing Jesus.

So I ask you today: Do you know Jesus? Do you have life in Him—
real, meaningful life? If you believe the words of Jesus in John 10:10,
then you already have everything that you need.

"The thief comes only to steal and kill and destroy; I have
come that they may have life, and have it to the full."
John 10:10

Perhaps you have never taken that first step. You acknowledge Jesus existed, but you stop short of knowing Him. I get it. How do you possibly connect with someone you cannot see? It starts with a simple thought, prayer, or statement. Maybe something like this:

> Jesus, I am just like Eve. I sometimes doubt that you
> are real, good, or that You care about me. I try to fix
> my problems on my own, but it just does not seem
> to work. I want real life. I believe that You can give
> me that real, meaningful life. I know that I cannot
> pay my own penalty, and so I admit that I give up. I
> need You to fix my mistakes and to forgive my sins. I
> believe that by dying on the cross, You took my place.
> Even if I don't understand everything now, I trust
> You, and I want to follow You. Amen.

The Bible says that if we believe with our hearts and confess with our mouths, we will be forgiven and restored. If you took that first step today toward knowing Jesus, can I be the first to whoop and holler with you? A new chapter in your life has begun. I cannot wait to hear what living life to the full looks like in your story!

"If you confess with your mouth that Jesus is Lord and believe in
your heart that God raised him from the dead, you will be saved."
Romans 10:9 (NLT)

Is This Real Life?

The temptation in American culture, and even in the Western church, is to make comfort the ultimate goal of our lives. Our pursuit is ease, safety, and security. But is that what Jesus meant by the abundant life?

All three of these can be wonderful blessings from the Lord, but none of them is a guarantee. In fact, He promised persecution, suffering, danger, and the opportunity to do great and courageous things in His name. But rather than embracing the life that He came to give, we see "life to the full" and associate it with two kids and a white picket fence. Jesus did not come to make the American dream a reality but to do the will of His Father. His desire was that none might be separated from God and that all might come to know Him. Somehow, we have muddled the message and lulled ourselves to sleep with Anthropologie catalogues and vacation packages.

Please do not hear me wrong. Desiring a romantic relationship is not wrong, but we must remember that marriage is not the culmination of this life. It is not the goal of our journey, and it is certainly not the climax of the story. The temptation is to buy into Hollywood's idea that a boyfriend, husband, or relationship will bring us ultimate satisfaction and happiness. That is so much pressure to put onto an imperfect person. I cannot fulfill a man any more than a man might do that for me. God is the only one who has the power to bring us to joyful completion.

We start living a good love story by *living* our lives rather than waiting for life to happen to us. I think I often became so weighed down with the desire to have a relationship that I forgot to actually *live my life!* Don't fall into that same trap. Remember that you are called to live, love, and believe right where you are. Plenty of men and women have lived single lives full of more love than some marriages will ever demonstrate.

> "And don't be wishing you were someplace else or with
> someone else. Where you are right now is God's place
> for you. Live and obey and love and believe right there.
> God, not your marital status, defines your life ..."
> *1 Corinthians 7:17 (MSG)*

While God doesn't promise ease or romantic perfection in our relationships, I do know we can trust God to make good on the promises He *has* made.

> "God is not human, that He should lie, not a human being, that He should change His mind. Does He speak and then not act? Does He promise and not fulfill?"
> *Numbers 23:19*

I did not share my prom story so that you can feel sorry for me. I tell you these things because I want you to learn from my mistakes. I happened to wait for my date, but I just as easily could have stayed home because I was worried about the way my body looked. We can all make excuses for stalling instead of living, but the truth is that Jesus didn't come to give us life *after* we get married. Jesus has given each of us an amazing opportunity and a unique calling on our lives right now.

Since my high school prom, God has laid my own words heavily on my heart. *"No one will ever want me. My life will never start."* Not only does Jesus want me, but He *loves* me and has given me real and full life right now. His love has given me the courage to live my story for Him.

So what are you waiting for, friend? Are you living your life, or do you believe the lie that real life starts when *this* or *that* happens? You don't need a corsage. You don't have to wait around. Everything He has for you is yours right now. He loves you. He sent His son Jesus to die for you. The Savior of all, the Messiah, the King of Kings came so that you might have real, meaningful life. When you know and believe this, everything will change.

Life in Jesus means the following:

» Your presence is on purpose.

11

» Your true identity is found in Him.

» You can trust Him with the desires of your heart.

» Your heart is worth protecting.

» You can embrace His perfect plans for your life.

» You can take courage to move from fear to faith.

» You can believe that His good *is* good.

> "And I pray that you, being rooted and established in love, may have power together with all the saints to grasp how wide and long and high and deep is the love of Christ, and to know this love that surpasses knowledge—that you may be filled to the measure of all the fullness of God."
> *Ephesians 3:17–19*

So what about you? Are you living, or are you waiting for your life to start?

My Journal Entry

April 20, 2005

I have prayed for so long to be simply satisfied in You and to one day have a family. I know—twenty-three years old doesn't seem that old, right? So many of my friends are married. I don't feel deficient—just sad for some reason. So why do weddings and love stories sadden me? Why do they make me feel large, loud, and unwanted? Why does Satan get in so easily? Help me out, Lord! I don't want to live life in the wings. I want to live!

Father, my heart thinks romantic love will make me feel wanted, desirable, complete, fulfilled, at peace, happy, content, and giddy. But I know these are all passing and fleeting compared to the love you bestow on me. So why is it so hard to believe that with everything in me? I still struggle with the idea that my future may not contain love in the marital sense, children in the literal sense, and fulfillment of my dreams. Help me to make my prayers and desires align with Your will instead of just my own.

Your Journal Entry

Chapter 2

Original

A heart at peace gives life to the body, but envy rots the bones.
Proverbs 14:30

Dear Fourth-Grade Ginger,

It's okay to get embarrassed. Accidents happen to all of us. It's okay to want a redo. But it's not okay to hide. Just remember that it doesn't matter what other people think. What really matters is what God thinks, and He loves that you are ridiculous and awkward. He loves you so very, very much.

Love,
Today's Ginger

Problem

I have a major problem. I don't really know who I am.

I'm not speaking in an "I hit my head and can't remember my name" kind of way. I know my name, age, and my address. I know my parents' middle names and my sister's phone number.

But if you took all that away and asked, "Who are you?" I might be hard-pressed to answer. That's because the answer changes every day and might even change several times within the *same* day. Who am I? No, really. *Who am I?* More importantly, am I my *real* self with anyone?

This inability to identify my true self is one of the big problems I have with self-esteem.

The definition of *self-esteem*, according to Dictionary.com, is this:

1. A realistic respect for or favorable impression of oneself; self-respect.

2. An inordinately or exaggeratedly favorable impression of oneself.[2]

Now compare that with what we read in Philippians 2:3, which says, "Do nothing out of selfish ambition or vain conceit, but in humility consider others better than yourselves." In humility, we are to consider others—everyone else—as better than us. This does not say to have a poor view of ourselves but to have merely a *right* view of who we are in God's eyes. We are His, but we are not better than each other.

Even if we totally ignore God and what He wants in this equation, I believe that we *still* have a problem!

Here is the issue I have with self-esteem. Although I oftentimes have *zero* trouble discovering an exaggeratedly favorable impression of myself, most days my self-esteem fluctuates almost hourly. The way I identify myself is directly connected to my emotions and feelings. Emotions change quickly. What we are feeling for a period of time, unless depression is involved, tends to change countless times throughout the day. That means I can be on cloud nine in the morning because I received an encouraging text from a friend, and the next minute I'm depressed about the quiz for which I forgot to study. Full of joy, I might just walk out the door in the morning only to trip in front of a really attractive guy and find myself in the pit of despair. Yes, a pit of despair.

The idea that I could work on or grow my self-esteem doesn't connect with me because I cannot maintain a favorable impression of myself for longer than ten minutes. I embarrass myself more times than I would like to admit. Let me share a favorite example from when I was in the fourth grade. (I can't believe I'm about to tell you this.)

I've always been mildly competitive. (Ahem.) Keyboarding class in fourth grade was no different. I was diligently plugging away, typing, "As, if, the, dog, did, sit, on, the, cat ..."

I happened to have a seat right next to one of the boys in my class that day. This particularly competitive gentleman was quick to issue me a speed-keyboarding challenge. As we began typing, I realized that I would soon need to take a trip to the ladies' room. Apparently, I had had too much to drink from the water fountain that day. But I was not about to let a boy beat me. I focused all my attention on level two of the game and upon winning.

That's when everything started to go downhill.

I really had to go to the restroom. Like *really*. So I decided to make a quick decision that might help me stay in the game *and* get some relief. I was going to keep typing, but I was also *going to go*—just a little bit—to help take the edge off.

Oh, Ginger. Bad call. Bad choice. Badly done. It was as if a dam broke and suddenly I was peeing in my seat—and there was no end in sight. I couldn't stop. Fourth-grade me was sitting in her denim skirt on a folding chair that was rapidly filling with warm liquid. It didn't take long for my competitor to notice that I slowed my typing. Everything after that point seemed to happen in slow motion. I can't remember it, but I also can't forget it. My eyes widened as he realized what I already knew: I had peed my pants.

I think I ran, although I did probably asked for permission to leave, since I am a perpetual rule-follower. I snagged my PE shorts from my backpack and hightailed it to the bathroom. I stayed in that bathroom for as long as I could. I leaned against a wall and cried. I did not want to go back to my classroom. I did not want to face that boy. Not only had he beaten me, but he had also witnessed the most embarrassing moment of my life.

I finally talked myself into making the long trek back to my classroom. It felt as though every head turned to look at me as I slowly took my seat. Luckily, my misery was short-lived. The bell rang and I booked it out of that school. I took my mortified self out to our carpool and quietly and painfully endured the ride home.

Once home, I buried my head in my pillow and informed my mom that I would never, never, never go back to school. I was done with education forever. I would have to be like one of the pioneers on the Oregon Trail and make my way at home with Ma and Pa. It wasn't the life I would have originally chosen, but then again, one had to make adjustments for bladder mishaps.

I cannot remember exactly what my mom said to me that day, but I do know that she encouraged me to face this embarrassing moment head on. She sat on my bed, listened through my tears, and then walked me through how I would indeed be returning to school the very next day. This moment did not have to define my future.

In retrospect, I wish my ten-year-old self had taken that message to heart. For a while, I chose to let my embarrassment chip away at every speck of self-esteem I contained. I wasn't even able to retell this story until I was about twenty years old. When I was in the eighth grade, another kid in my class asked me what had actually happened on that fateful day. I had such a "favorable impression" of myself that I was able to respond confidently, "I had serious bladder issues at that time. Doctors thought it might have been an infection. Yeah. It was pretty bad. I almost had to have surgery." *False*.

The thing is, I have embarrassing escapades on a daily basis! Fourth grade is one thing, but your freshman year in college is quite another. One day I was jogging around campus with the hope of seeing a particular guy who had caught my attention. I took a path around the perimeter of campus with the intention of locating his car. *If* I saw his car, I would need to make a stop at the post office, since he happened to work there.

At the end of my run, I came around the side of the building and hopped up onto a little ledge that surrounded the patio. I started running on the foot-wide ledge. First of all, I'm not particularly coordinated. Secondly, the ledge was a good three feet above the paved ground. Long story short, I took a wrong step and ate the pavement. It completely knocked the wind out of me. Luckily, there was only a couple making out and a group of fraternity brothers gathered to witness my fall, but I assured everyone that the best course of action would be to merely laugh *with* me. See me laugh. Ha. Ha.

Like I said, I am well versed in the art of embarrassment. I know.

You're thinking that I just need to learn to laugh at myself. I do that too. But sometimes, I let the hurt get the best of me. I'm an emotional being. The reason I don't have fuzzy, warm feelings toward the concept of self-esteem is because I am prone to change and I am (at times) an emotional wreck! However, my heavenly Father says He loves me infinitely, and He never changes. As hard as it may be to believe, it's absolutely the truth.

Comparison

We all do it.

How do I stack up? How do I compare with all of my friends or with other girls? Are my clothes worthy of the runway? Do I look good enough to be noticed? Am I thin enough? Will I fit in?

Comparison reveals a lot of our insecurities. I worked at a Christian camp during the summers of my college years. I was excited for new friends, counseling preteens, and hopefully meeting a godly, Christian guy. What I wasn't expecting was how insecure I felt that first summer. Most of the counselors attended state universities and had tiny runner's bodies. Several of them had worked previous summers, so they already had established relationships. It was a very intimidating situation. I was outside the loop from day one—or so I thought. I didn't know how to break in. I felt like I was in high school all over again, with an "A" crowd that wouldn't accept new members.

But there was one girl in particular with whom I directly compared myself. This beautiful girl had worked the first half of the summer and was in thick with the "A" crowd. They went to the lake on the weekends, had tons of inside jokes, and were genuinely wonderful people. So of course I let myself feel wounded by them and by her.

Mia was lovely, funny, and liked by everyone. She had been convinced by her friends to remain for the second half of the summer, which just so happened to be my half. I found myself thinking, *She's not supposed to be here.* I was being ridiculous. I was hurt when she was selected to participate in lunch skits while I was the one pursuing a theater degree. I was upset when she was assigned to come and teach the high-ropes activity class with me, even though she was substituting for a sick counselor. Because I felt threatened by her, I compared myself to her, and ultimately I resented her. But the truth is I wanted to *be* her. The more I compared, the less joy I experienced in my work.

Amazing how that works, isn't it? Comparison is the thief of joy. It's true. I've proved it time and again in my own life. Let me say that one more time. *Comparison is the thief of joy.*

God has creative ways of teaching us the lessons we are hesitant to learn. The next summer, I showed up for my assignment at camp and was paired with none other than Mia. We were scheduled to teach an activity class together and spent close to six hours a day, five days a week, for six weeks in a row lifeguarding at the pool. This, of course, allowed us to become really great friends that summer. It was amazing to see how God was reminding me that He loved us *both* and had uniquely created each of us. I learned so much that summer when I turned my hurt and comparison over to the Lord and prayed specifically for Mia as we spent time with one another.

In the last verses of the gospel of John, we find an interesting story about my favorite disciple, Peter. Peter, the "speak first, think later" disciple, was given a unique and individual call.

> "Feed my lambs … Take care of my sheep … Feed my sheep."
> *John 21:15–17*

I don't know how I would have responded, but Peter makes me wince. "Peter turned and saw that the disciple whom Jesus loved was following them ... When Peter saw him, he asked, 'Lord, what about him?'" (John 21:20–21). Peter immediately turned and compared his calling with the one Jesus had given to John. I wince because I am prone to the exact same pattern of behavior. Rather than responding with humility and gratitude, I flippantly lament my looks, calling, and life. I pull a Peter every single day.

Peter was given the calling that he alone was created to live out. Peter could not be John. John could not be Peter. But like Peter, I am so sure that if only I could have *her* platform, popularity, or position, *then* I could find my joy. "Lord, what about her?"

Jesus responds to you and me in the same way he responds to Peter. "Jesus answered, 'If I want him to remain alive until I return, what is that to you? You must follow me'" (John 21:22).

When we compare our calling to anyone else's, we take our eyes off the source of our joy. That's why comparison is the thief of joy. Comparison keeps my eyes off the one who is calling my name. If we want to live and run this race with endurance, we need to keep our eyes on Jesus.

"Therefore, since we are surrounded by such a huge crowd of witnesses
to the life of faith, let us strip off every weight that slows us down,
especially the sin that so easily trips us up. And let us run with
endurance the race God has set before us. We do this by keeping our
eyes on Jesus, the champion who initiates and perfects our faith."
Hebrews 12:1–2 (NLT)

Peter listened in that moment on the Sea of Galilee. Something clicked. He spent the rest of his life with tunnel vision and the call of Jesus ringing through his ears: "You must follow me."

Peter challenges us all in his first letter. "Each one should use whatever gift he has received to serve others, faithfully administering God's grace in its various forms" (1 Peter 4:10).

Galatians 6:3–5 in The Message translation has some direct words when it comes to comparing ourselves with others. It reads,

> Live creatively, friends ... Make a careful exploration of who you are and the work you have been given, and then sink yourself into that. Don't be impressed with yourself. Don't compare yourself with others. Each of you must take responsibility for doing the creative best you can with your own life.

Rather than being caught up with wishing you could be more like someone else, take the challenge from Galatians and do the creative best you can with your own life. You are unique and original—and so am I. Peter wasn't created to be John. And for me to try to be like Mia would have been wasted energy. Let's not spend time conforming to an original, because you'll just be a copy. And really, who wants to live that way?

Masterpiece

Psalm 139 says that I am "fearfully and wonderfully made." It tells me that God formed me and wove me together in my mother's womb even before she knew that she was going to have a child. He chose my green eyes and my frustrating eyebrows, which seem to have a mind of their own. He chose my dishwater hair color, my body type, and my height. Yet too often, I carelessly comment about how He formed me.

We are quick to criticize the size of our thighs, the length of our noses, and even the shape of our toes! The words *fearfully* and *wonderfully* express the gentleness and tenderness with which we were created. Have you ever held an infant before? Better yet, have you ever seen someone who is reluctant to hold a baby? It is generally not because they dislike babies but rather because they fear hurting them. They recognize that something so fragile requires tender care. God showed ultimate tenderness as He formed us. David wonders at God's care when he says in Psalm 8:3, "When I consider Your heavens, the work of Your fingers, the moon and the stars, which You have set in place."

Why mention the stars when talking about how God created us? Read it again. The universe is the work of God's *fingers*! There is no part of us that was casually or thoughtlessly formed. If He perfectly placed flaming balls of gas and magma into the sky, what does that say about how He created you and me? He declares you to be His *poema*, His poem, His masterpiece. Not only that, but He continues to think on us even after He creates us! "How precious are your thoughts about me, O God. They cannot be numbered!" (Psalm 139:17 NLT) God not only created you as the crown of His creation, but He thinks innumerable precious thoughts *about* you!

Why are we are so eager to criticize His creation? Check out God's perspective in Isaiah 29:16. "You are confused. You think the clay is equal to the potter. You think that an object can tell the one who made it, 'You didn't make me.' This is like a pot telling its maker, 'You don't know anything.'"

Often, I stand in front of my mirror and think, *I know I'm supposed to like what I see, but God, You don't really know anything about what it takes to be pretty.* We play the role of clay talking back to our "Potter" on a daily basis.

Imagine I am an artist and I decide to paint the setting sun. I set up my paints and stand out on my balcony to watch a beautiful Arizona sunset. I carefully select my colors and work for days to complete my masterpiece. On the fourth day of painting, I hear a voice. "Orange," it says. At first, I don't believe I hear it. I continue with the purple on my brush, but soon I can't deny the sound. "Orange!" It's coming from my canvas, complaining that I haven't included enough orange in my masterpiece.

That would be quite a feat! As a writer, I acknowledge that my art does speak to me, but it's never in the audible sense. The artist, not the art, has the final opinion on the finished product. Yet that's exactly what we say to God on a regular basis. "I wish I was skinnier. I hate my chin. Why do I have so many stupid freckles? And why do my eyebrows hate me?" Ridiculous but true.

God chose you as dearly loved. He did not carelessly make you. He did not fling you from heaven to earth. He gently and wonderfully made you as His beautiful work of art. Step into the masterpiece you were created to be.

Valuable

God is very specific in the Bible concerning how He feels about us. In fact, the next chapters of this book are devoted to God's thoughts about you. I'll give you a hint: His thoughts are good. Really good. But we have a problem, you and I.

How God sees us *should* be the only opinion that matters—after all, He made us. *He made us!* Since we are His daughters, our identity should only be found in how He values us. He made us and loved us enough to give us free will, the choice to love Him or leave Him.

Let's go back to the very beginning and get the story straight. God created us. It started in the garden of Eden with Adam and Eve. He gave them everything and told them simply to "enjoy!" Sin entered the picture, and as a result, Adam and Eve (and the rest of us from there on out) were exposed to death. We were separated from the God who created us. The penalty for Adam and Eve's sin, and our sin, is death;

the payment is blood. Thankfully, our Father considered us valuable enough to buy us back.

Think about it this way: we determine the value of something by how much we are willing to spend. If I walk into a store intending to buy a flat iron, without having done any research on flat irons, I'm limited to two things: what the box says and how much the flat iron costs. Of course, the box is going to talk up the product. I have yet to see the company gutsy enough to print, "Fairly decent flat iron. Let's face it: you're paying twenty dollars for this, so don't get your hopes up." So if I can't trust a box to tell me something more than the voltage and information about a warranty, I have to go by price. I immediately rule out the cheapest brand, and *if* I have the money, I will probably take the top of the line. Why? The price indicates that this flat iron is *worth* the extra money. The value of the flat iron is indicated by the expense. While I may not be willing to spend $185 on a new flat iron, I certainly might be prepared to pay that amount for some new photo-editing software. I place a higher value on my photos than a flat iron. Let's face it: my hair is already straight as a stick.

God deemed us not only valuable enough to create in the first place but also priceless enough to buy us back! Do you know how frustrating it is to lose something you just bought? I seem to do that with new pens. I have a certain kind I like for grip, writing ease, and ink flow. I get a package of three, and sooner than I would like, they're gone. I'd like to believe I've misplaced them, but I know that my coworkers sometimes just need a pen and they reach for one off my desk. I don't think anyone intentionally steals my pens; I just think they forget to put them back. But imagine my frustration if I watch someone take and use my pen and then only agree to give it back *if* I pay them a fee. I already paid for *my* pen once; no way I'm doing that again—especially if they raise the price.

God proved how much He valued us by what He was willing to spend. I'm notorious for shouting the phrase, "Prove it!" to my friends when they make a bold statement. Usually, I'm joking around, but sometimes, I want them to put their money where their mouth is. "I can run a five-minute mile!" My response? "Prove it!"

You can shout "Prove it!" all you want, and He will always have the best response ready for you. Remember He already owned us once before. He bought us *again* with the life and death of His only son, Jesus. Jesus had done nothing to deserve punishment, yet He died in our place. He died for me. He died for you. The cost of that sacrifice shows that you are a priceless treasure of the King of Kings. The gift of His son demonstrates God's great love for us!

> "But God demonstrates His own love for us in this:
> While we were still sinners, Christ died for us."
> *Romans 5:8*

My perception of self-esteem shifts and changes all the time. (Wait, it just did again. Awesome.) But God's perception never will. Self-esteem would have me working hard to *feel* better, but I now know that until my worth is centered upon God's redeeming act of love, my feelings will fluctuate like a washing machine out of balance. Our center of gravity must be the truth found in God's Word and *not* human emotion. Regardless of our feelings, we are valuable and unique masterpieces for whom God proved His love once and for all.

So the choice is yours. You can spend a lifetime trying to accept yourself and artificially raise your self-esteem, or you can know Him, the one who masterfully created you.

> "I will give them a heart to know me, that I am the
> LORD. They will be my people, and I will be their God,
> for they will return to me with all their heart."
> *Jeremiah 24:7*

Do you believe that your presence is on purpose? What do
you believe will give you a sense of identity and purpose?

My Journal Entry

January 30, 2005

"There's such a lot of different Annes in me. I sometimes think that is why I'm such a troublesome person. If I was just the one Anne it would be ever so much more comfortable, but then it wouldn't be half so interesting."

L. M. Montgomery, *Anne of Green Gables* [3]

I feel the same way today. I have so many interests, so many different friends. Who am I? No, *really*. Who am I, and am I my genuine self with anyone? Father, I am tired of running, worrying, hoping, and searching. I desire Your approval, timing, and answers alone. Please help make that my reality, any way You like.

People keep telling me to "wait," as if telling a child to wait their turn. But deep inside, I feel like a child. I don't really want what they have; I just don't want them to be happier than me. I sound like a horrible person. "Hey, since you are so happy with your diamond and white dress, I can't be your friend." Too many people with white dresses and too much loneliness in a car full of people.

Your Journal Entry

CHAPTER 3

Knowing

You will seek me and find me when you seek me with all your heart.
Jeremiah 29:13

Dear Twenty-Two-Year-Old Ginger,

I understand where you are coming from. You are desperately hoping God will tell you exactly what to do with your life when you graduate. You keep begging Him to shout the answer to you, but the truth is that He has *already spoken*. Where can you possibly go and not honor Him with your life? Just put one foot in front of the other and trust that He's powerful enough to keep you on course.

Love,
Today's Ginger

Abstract Art

"To thine own self be true."[4]

Do you have any idea where I can find this verse in the Bible? Maybe in Psalms, Proverbs, or Ecclesiastes?

I'll give you a hint: Polonius, not Solomon, spoke those words. The line is actually from *Hamlet*, by William Shakespeare. Shakespeare and many others would have us believe that our ultimate life pursuit should be to completely and fully know ourselves. I myself set out on a European adventure one semester in college in the hope that somehow, some way, I would return home more sure of who I was. I spent a lot of time searching and sightseeing, and while I returned home with stories and pictures, I couldn't identify *my own self* with any more confidence than when I had left home.

If you search in the Bible for a verse that echoes Shakespeare's plea to be true to oneself, you simply won't find it. But do you know what you *will* discover on many pages of the Bible? Know *God* more. In Psalm 46:10, God reminds us to stop all the striving. "Be still, and know that I am God; I will be exalted among the nations, I will be exalted in the earth."

Jeremiah 9:23–24 dispels the rumor of greatness originating from self-exploration.

> This is what the Lord says: "Let not the wise man boast of his wisdom or the strong man boast of his strength or the rich man boast of his riches, but let him who boasts boast about this: *that he understands and knows me,* that I am the Lord, who exercises kindness, justice and righteousness on earth, for in these I delight," declares the Lord.
>
> (emphasis added)

Have you ever visited an art museum? I enjoy spending an afternoon wandering through galleries, but sometimes in the abstract-art section, I really wish the artist would show up and explain his or her work. I want to understand the intention behind the paintings that confuse me. I very rarely comprehend or fully appreciate abstract art. But if you don't understand something, the best person to explain the work is typically the one who made it.

I set out on the "know myself" journey, and it left me more confused than before. God knows us better than we know ourselves. I need His perspective, because I do not trust my own self. At my core, my heart just cannot be trusted.

Have you ever heard the phrase, "Follow your heart"? Or "Trust your heart"? Maybe "Go with your gut"? Sometimes, especially if you are a Disney princess, this can be a great plan. But here's what Jeremiah says about our pure and lovely hearts: "The heart is deceitful and beyond a cure. Who can understand it?" That's the New International Version, but check out the New Living Translation: "The human heart is the most deceitful of all things, and desperately wicked. Who really knows how bad it is?" (Jeremiah 17:9).

That sounds really bad, doesn't it? Jeremiah is saying that our hearts, left on their own, are deceitful and wicked. Within every Little Mermaid, there's a sea witch waiting inside. Within every Cinderella, there's a wicked stepmother waiting to come out, especially when we've had a bad day, are more tired than usual, or cannot seem to catch a break.

Remember my story about my friend Mia, the fellow counselor from my summer camp? My heart was so hardened toward her that I could feel the envy pulsating from me. But when I began to see the special way God had made *each* of us, I slowly released my hurt to the Lord. I was finally able to recognize the true nature of my heart. I started praying that God would change my heart and show me how I could best love and serve Mia. And as I mentioned before, God worked in my stubborn heart in such a powerful way that Mia and I ended up being very close friends that summer.

God alone has the power to change our hearts. It becomes very challenging to resent someone when you are sincerely praying that God would pour out good things on him or her. Try it. Try it with the girls in your class, the women at your workplace, and even the stars and celebrities on TV. It could be that the anger you feel toward certain women is actually a strong indication that there is something much deeper going on inside of your heart.

Garbage In, Garbage Out

"The good man brings good things out of the good stored up in his heart, and the evil man brings evil things out of the evil stored up in his heart. For out of the overflow of his heart his mouth speaks." That's Jesus speaking in Luke 6:45. It's easy to breeze through this verse and not really let the truth penetrate.

A dear friend and spiritual mentor from my summer camp put it this way:

> Imagine you come to our house and ask for a cup of hot coffee. We pour it into a mug for you, and maybe you pour in some creamer until liquid fills the cup to the brim. The coffee is on the verge of spilling. You slowly walk to take a seat on the couch when all of a sudden one of our kids runs through the room and bumps your elbow. No matter how good your reflexes are, you are going to spill. So even as you try to shield the cup, liquid is going to pour out over the side of the cup and cover you or my kid. And in this moment,

that's going to be hot coffee. If any other liquid were
to come out of the cup, it would be a total surprise.

Every day we interact with many people, and every day we have the
chance of being bumped, so to speak. Whatever we are filled with is
going to spill over and onto others. So what's it going to be?

Think about the last time you said something you wish you hadn't.
Perhaps it was a mean word to a friend, a passive-aggressive remark to
a coworker, or an ungrateful response to a parent. Have you ever said
something you regretted and then thought (or said), *Where did that
come from?* Jesus makes the source of our words very clear in Matthew
12:34. "For out of the overflow of the heart the mouth speaks." The
answer is inside us. Proverbs 27:19 says, "As water reflects a face, so a
man's heart reflects the man." Tie both of these ideas together, and
we get a complete picture. Your words and thoughts come out of your
heart, and your heart reflects you as a woman. As women, what does
this mean for all of us?

Music, movies, conversations, television—everything we put into our
hearts ultimately determines what comes out of our mouths and is
expressed through our actions. Garbage in, garbage out. If we want
pure and good things to flow from our mouths and thoughts, we have
to fill up with the good stuff. I cannot put hot coffee in my cup and
then expect to see cold water spill out. The surest way to change how
we respond to the people we resent, dislike, fear, or envy is to speak
and think good things over them.

Have you ever trained for a race or increased your level of exercise? At
first, you don't want to run or go to the gym, but eventually, you crave
exercise and miss it on the days when it doesn't fit in your schedule.
If blessing those who you compare yourself with is hard to swallow,
keep at it. Remember your thoughts and words reflect your heart, and
your heart reflects you.

Know Him

Clearly, I don't know if I want to trust myself. My heart is pretty rotten. But thankfully, God is always in the business of changing us from the inside out. He desires for us to find real and lasting heart change—transformation that happens by spending time in His presence. That is why it's so important to listen to and know God's words. **Who I am is constantly changing, but *He* is not.** "I the Lord do not change. So you, O descendants of Jacob, are not destroyed" (Malachi 3:6).

So what do we do?

We *seek* Him. We *know Him* more.

Let's head back to Jeremiah again. "You will seek me and find me when you seek me with all your heart" (Jeremiah 29:13).

Great. So I am supposed to seek God with my whole deceitful heart? How do I do that?

A few years ago, I heard a tale about a young man who asked the very same question of an older, wiser man in his village.

The wise man told the young man to go and fill a bucket with water. The young man quickly did so and then returned the filled bucket to the wise man and waited expectantly for instruction. The older man instructed the boy to place his entire head in the water and then to be completely still. The young man obeyed and plunged his head below the surface of the cold water.

But as he did this, the older man suddenly came up behind him and held the boy's head firmly under the water. The young man struggled, but the old man did not relent. Just as the boy was about to pass out, the wise man finally removed his hand and allowed the boy to raise his head and gasp for breath. The young boy struggled for air and fell back to the ground to rest.

The wise man looked him squarely in the eye and said, "That is how you seek God. You want Him as much as that first gulp of breath you just took."

Filling Up

> "Draw near to God and He will draw near to you."
> *James 4:8*

God desires to spend time with you. He tells us to seek Him. I think one of the best places to start spending time with God is in His Word, the Bible. *I can't recommend this enough.* If I could take each of you and shake your shoulders right now, I would. I would not even care how weird that might seem. When it comes to hearing from God, His Word is the primary source and it is a filter for the messages that bombard our hearts and minds each day. God's Word is like a megaphone to His people. We recognize His voice best when we spend time listening to what He has to say through the Bible on a regular basis.

But I think most people (myself included) don't invest the time in our relationship with God because we just don't want to put forth the effort. We start to read the Bible but find it confusing. We try to pray but end up feeling discouraged when we can't remain focused. We spend our time with God going through the motions rather than enjoying His presence.

I have found that many Christians are very familiar with Jeremiah 29:11. I have a picture frame with the verse on it. "'For I know the plans I have for you,' declares the Lord, 'plans to prosper you and not to harm you, plans to give you hope and a future.'" Nice verse! It's an extremely comforting promise for us to claim, but keep reading. "'Then you will call upon me and come and pray to me, and I will listen to you. You will seek me and find me when you seek me with all your heart. I will be found by you,' declares the Lord" (Jeremiah 29:11–14a).

In this particular passage, God is actually speaking to His chosen people: Israel. After their time of discipline, God promises that He will restore them when they seek Him with all their heart. So how can these verses apply to you and me today?

Intimacy with God requires effort, but there are a million things on any given day competing for our time. If our desire is to know Him more, then we need to do whatever we can to focus our attention. Author and speaker Hayley DiMarco makes a great point when she says, "You cannot seek anyone with all your heart in your spare time."[5] Isn't that the truth! When we spend time with the Lord, we need to avoid distractions. An easy first step is to turn off phones and close computers. Even if that time is just in the shower, give Him your full attention in that moment.

Don't let yourself get discouraged if you aren't growing as fast as you might like. Just keep moving forward. Remember that walking is still moving. Some days, I can read a whole book of the Bible in one sitting, and other days, I can only manage a quick prayer. Pick it back up tomorrow. Do not let guilt keep you away from the gift of God's presence.

> "But as for you, be strong and do not give up,
> for your work will be rewarded."
> *2 Chronicles 15:7*

If you are like me, you may allow *serving* God to replace actually *knowing* Him. Instead of spending time with God praying or reading the Bible, we often try to do many things so God will love us more. But here's the deal: God cannot love us any more or any less than He does right now. His love is not earned; it's freely given!

Ephesians 2:9–10 in the New Living Translation reminds us, "Salvation is not a reward for the good things we have done, so none of us can boast about it. For we are God's masterpiece. He has created us anew in Christ Jesus, so we can do the good things he planned for us long ago."

When He looks at you, He sees the beautiful woman He formed before she was born. He desires our hearts far more than any sacrifice or work. Hosea 6:6 in the New Living Translation says, "I want you to show love, not offer sacrifices. I want you to know me more than I want burnt offerings."

Mark 6:31 does not say, "Come with me by yourselves to a quiet place and get to work." It says, "Come with me by yourselves to a quiet place and get some *rest*."

Did you realize it was Jesus speaking in that verse? Jesus took time to go off by Himself and pray. This particular time, He fills up on prayer before He feeds five thousand people with just five loaves of bread and two fish. Jesus demonstrates taking a break to spend time with His Father over and over again in the New Testament. His example should compel us to fill up on God's presence. But rather than responding like Jesus, all too often we turn to just about anything else to satisfy our cravings. Let me give you an example.

My favorite snack in the world is chips and salsa. I typically arrive at Mexican restaurants absolutely starving. I take my seat at the table, and as soon as that first basket of chips hits the table, I am in heaven! I eat through the first basket and finish up most of the second before I realize that I am not going to have any room for my shrimp tacos.

Tortilla chips may fill me up for a while, but they certainly won't satisfy or sustain me for long. Darn you, chips and salsa! I just got stuffed on starch when the feast was waiting for me. It's the same thing with our relationship with God. If we fill up on celebrity gossip, social media, the latest show, music, or our boyfriend, we often don't have time or energy left for the banquet of God's Word. It's not that we can't or shouldn't enjoy those things, but the way we spend our time very clearly indicates our priorities. Are we filling up on things that will never be able to satisfy our soul?

Isaiah 55:2 reads, "Why spend money on what is not bread, and your labor on what does not satisfy? Listen, listen to me, and eat what is good, and your soul will delight in the richest of fare."

I find it interesting that we must *listen* in order to eat what is good. That tells me that God's Word is food for my hungering soul. God's portion isn't stingy. Forget the picture of stale bread and dirty water. Throw that image out of your mind. God's Word is compared to good food and the richest of fare! It's filling, satisfying, and overflowing. Why would a God who loves to give good gifts fill us with anything less? Oh, that we would "taste and see that the Lord is good" (Psalm 34:8).

This world is full of amazing diversions, but I think we know in our hearts that there must be more than simply drinking coffee and checking status updates. We are all at one of two places. We have either entered into a relationship with God *or* we are still debating whether or not to accept His proposal. Regardless of your relationship status with God at this point, I can't encourage you enough to take the time to get to know your creator. My hope and prayer is that the more time you spend getting to know your heavenly Father, the more confident and joyful you will be in that relationship. God welcomes us to trade in our confusion and emptiness for what will really satisfy.

> "I pray that from his glorious, unlimited resources he will empower
> you with inner strength through his Spirit. Then Christ will
> make his home in your hearts as you trust in him. Your roots
> will grow down into God's love and keep you strong. And may
> you have the power to understand, as all God's people should,
> how wide, how long, how high, and how deep his love is."
> *Ephesians 3:16–18 (NLT)*

Every day, we choose whether we will fill up on carbs or make our way to the banquet table that holds the real feast of God's presence. I want to feel the way about God's Word that I do about food. I want to crave it, thirst for it, hunger after it. I'm so thankful He loves to answer this prayer: "Lord, let me love Your Word." If the Word still hasn't whet your appetite, can I challenge and invite you to pray this prayer today?

"Lord, let me love Your Word."

Anyone There?

Perhaps you do desire to connect with God but find yourself feeling like you can't hear Him. I've been there, done that, and have all the T-shirts.

During my senior year of college, I was tied up in worry knots. I kept asking God to show me exactly what to do after graduation. I felt like I had endless options, but I only wanted one: His best. So I made a plan. I wasn't hearing God audibly, so I decided to take a lesson from Elijah. In 1 Kings 19, Elijah expects to find God in the storm, in the fire, and in the earthquake. Instead, God reveals Himself in a gentle whisper.

> The Lord said, "Go out and stand on the mountain in the presence of
> the Lord, for the Lord is about to pass by." Then a great and powerful
> wind tore the mountains apart and shattered the rocks before the

Lord, but the Lord was not in the wind. After the wind there was an earthquake, but the Lord was not in the earthquake. After the earthquake came a fire, but the Lord was not in the fire. And after the fire came a gentle whisper. When Elijah heard it, he pulled his cloak over his face and went out and stood at the mouth of the cave.

1 Kings 19:11–13

I too wanted to hear God's whisper. I attempted to recreate the story of Elijah by quieting myself. I tried driving my car out into the middle of a field, opening the sunroof, and gazing at the stars. For all of my focus, I could only hear the crickets and the sound of distant cars rumbling on the highway. Then I tried going in my closet, opening my Bible, and pointing at random verses, but I still didn't get the response I was seeking.

I even ventured to a spot on my campus called The Quiet Place. Someone had donated small rooms with sparse furniture and comforting fountain noises to the students of the university in hopes that we would take Jesus at His Word; we would follow Him and get some rest. I took my journal and Bible into The Quiet Place, shut the door and lay on the floor. I closed my eyes and began to pray. I prayed hard. I prayed aloud, and I prayed quietly. I pleaded with God, "Tell me what to do already!" And as I quieted myself in that quiet place, do you know what He said? He said, "I'm not hiding!"

Okay, so He did not audibly say that. I didn't even end up blindly pointing to a verse in the Bible that said as much. Instead, I tried to wait patiently and just kept my eyes and ears open for the last weeks of my senior year. I prayed, read my Bible, and sought advice from godly people in my life. Slowly but surely, I began to realize that God really wasn't hiding.

Have you ever heard of the game sardines? I used to play it all the time as a kid. It's almost a reverse of traditional hide-and-seek." In sardines, the "it" person goes to hide and *everyone else* counts. Then everyone heads out looking for the person. If I find the sardine, I have to try to hide *with* that person in their hiding place. This continues until there is only one man left standing.

I'm sure you're wondering what this has to do with anything.

For a long time—especially in high school and college—I thought of my relationship with God as a game of sardines. I wanted to know God's will for my life so desperately, but I felt that no matter how hard I asked or looked, I just couldn't determine what God wanted for me. I would look at all of my friends, confidently making decisions, and couldn't help but think they had all found the answer. That was it—the entire world was hiding with God in a huge game of sardines, and I was the last one standing as they all told each other, "*Shhhhh.*"

"Everyone else can find You, so why can't I?" I would lose heart and resign myself to being last. That's crazy, right?

I feel like that every once in a while, even to this day. I've read and memorized Jeremiah 29:13 until it's practically a daily saying: "You will seek me and find me when you seek me with all your heart."

Mark Batterson, in his book *In a Pit with a Lion on a Snowy Day,* writes, "God wants you to get where God wants you to go, more than you want to get where God wants you to go."[6] We can use up a lot of energy worrying that we aren't hearing from God, or we can realize that if we are seeking Him in faith, He desires to be found by us.

This was the truth echoed by my college mentor when I shared the angst I was feeling about making my grown-up life decisions. Through tears, I explained to her my deep desire to know God's will for my future. I listed all the reasons why He should tell me exactly which job to take: I could obey Him quickly, I could stop worrying about this, I could spend more time praying about other things, etc. When I finally stopped talking, she met my gaze and asked, "But what takes more faith: an arrow that says, 'Go right here' or taking steps each day to draw closer to Him? Your desire is to honor God with your heart, gifts, and talents. Where can you possibly end up in this world and not be able to do that?"

My tears stopped and my head cleared. Hebrews 11:1 became my mantra each day. "And without faith it is impossible to please God, because anyone who comes to him must believe that he exists and that he rewards those who earnestly seek him."

Is God able to tell us exactly where and when to go? Absolutely. He does this countless times in Scripture and even does so audibly. But does that mean He will speak to each of us that way in every situation? Probably not. If your heart is attuned to Your Father and His given commands in the Bible, then step forward in faith even when you can't see or hear His answer. You have the Holy Spirit inside of you, and His Word to guide you. Make a decision, and go.

I think it is so encouraging to look through the Bible and remember how uniquely God speaks and calls to each of us. Moses saw God face-to-face; Paul got a light from heaven; Ezekiel watched dry bones; Gideon was visited by an angel; Elijah witnessed the fire, felt the quake, and then found God in the whisper; and still others were met by talking donkeys and storms that held them at bay. The important point is that you are seeking. When you desire to be in God's will, He *honors* that. When the Israelites finally sought God, "He was found by them" (2 Chronicles 15:15).

I have to keep reminding myself that God has given us everything we need to connect with Him. There aren't hidden tools to pick up as we age or mature. Spiritual growth isn't like passing levels on a video game. All the parts are included; every piece of the puzzle arrived in the box. From the outset, you and I are equipped to not only survive in this life but to thrive in our relationship with our heavenly Father.

Remember the following:

» He's not holding out on you, waiting for you to get it together.

» He sees you, and He hears you.

» His promises are precious and great.

» He loves you, and He has given you everything that you need to know Him.

> "His divine power has given us everything we need for life
> and godliness through our knowledge of him who called us
> by his own glory and goodness. Through these he has given
> us his very great and precious promises, so that through
> them you may participate in the divine nature and escape
> the corruption in the world caused by evil desires."
> *2 Peter 1:3–4*

We can take joy and peace from knowing God isn't hiding. He is waiting for us to seek Him. So even though Shakespeare and the rest of the world are pushing for us to know and praise *ourselves* more, God reassures us that we will find our true selves when we know and praise *Him* alone.

Even when I doubt my looks, compare myself to others, or have the most embarrassing moments, He *still* loves me. He continues to love me even when I let comparison steal my joy. He stands beside me and reminds me I am a work in progress and I am His. On our best days and our worst days, He loves us!

He made you. He bought you. He wants you. He'll have you. He picked you. He chose you. He hears you. He remembers you. He sees you. You belong to Him. When you seek Him with all your heart, you will find Him right where He's always been: waiting for you.

"My heart says of you, 'Seek his face.' Your face, LORD, I will seek."
Psalm 27:8

Who are you? Do you believe that your identity is found in God or in your accomplishments, relationships, or appearance?

My Journal Entry

September 4, 2006

Father, why have I stopped seeking Your face again? Do I really think the Internet holds all of the answers to what I am searching for? Could I not simply ask You for guidance and seek Your face?

You say in Your Word that when we seek You, we will find You when we seek with all our hearts. Father, if nothing else, I long for a heart focused on You. Father, guide my thoughts and my search. I will go wherever You call me. Guide me. I'm asking for it!

Your Journal Entry

Chapter 4

Desire

Delight yourself in the Lord and he will
give you the desires of your heart.
Psalm 37:4

Dear Twenty-Year-Old Ginger,

I know you aren't telling God what you really want. I get it. You want
to protect it. If you don't say it aloud, then you don't have a chance of
being disappointed. But taking your heartache into your own hands is
going to have disastrous results. Trust His timing and His good will
for you. Open up your hands, and let go. Let Him give you His best.

Love,
Today's Ginger

Girls Chase Boys

I spent my elementary years anticipating recess. Recess is even better than lunch; it's total freedom. I didn't generally run out to the playground to master the monkey bars or school someone in hopscotch. I reveled in that half hour because of one game in particular: girls chase boys.

If you aren't familiar with the particulars of the game, let me be the first to inform you. A female shouts out, "Girls chase boys!" As soon as she sounds the war cry, the males begin to run. The females scurry off trying to tag as many of them as possible. They tag and they tag until there is just one boy left in the game. He has the ability to say the words that every young girl longed to hear, "Switch! Boys chase girls!" At this point, the girls fly off in a hurry, hoping to not be caught by any of the boys who are now free to move about the play area. Whether I was being chased or doing the chasing, I had one target in mind: Evan Thompson. Evan was my first love—from kindergarten until he broke my heart and moved to Chicago in third grade. (Sad day. I still can't talk about it.)

This whole game involved a lot of running and screaming but not much in the way of winning. I have no idea how you would actually win boys chase girls or girls chase boys, because either side could declare a switch at any time. When I try to remember details, all I can really see is a flash of blonde hair. What I do know is that being chased by Evan could turn a good day into a great day.

I think my fascination with Evan began after I was so bold as to kiss him on the neck in kindergarten. Pretty daring for me, seeing as I have trouble making eye contact with the opposite sex on most occasions. I was smitten. My friends and I made code names for Evan and would often discuss how great "Nice" was. I think I was practicing "Mrs. Ginger Thompson" in my notebook by the time I was eight years old.

But then Evan and his family moved away and we didn't play our running games anymore. As fourth graders, we were much too mature for such things and proceeded to play the daring game of cootie crusaders. Again, I don't recall the details, but I'm sure it was entertaining for the teachers to watch.

I wish I could say that I left all of my chasing games in grade school. But I didn't. As I moved on to my public high school, I brought girls chase boys with me in hopes that one day the guy would say, "Switch!" and I would find myself running like mad.

Shoe Wars

Fast forward to my junior year of high school and I was following a blond California boy around the school. Masked in the cloak of friendship, I convinced myself that it was only a matter of time before Jay would realize that the love of his life was, in fact, standing right in front of him. My own infatuation played itself out in various arenas, but most notably in the hours following the final bell of the day. When I wasn't expected to remain after school for various rehearsals, I maneuvered to be in the fine arts building at the close of the day. I conveniently met up with Jay and spent many an afternoon either chatting in the back of his small pickup truck or enjoying a laugh in the choir room. In fact, I am pretty sure we spent several afternoons throwing our shoes at each other. I was so coy and clever. *That's the way to snag a boy, Ginger. Just throw things at him.* Many shoe wars later, I was faced with the undeniable fact that Jay was dating someone else. During the three years I was captivated by Jay, he dated three different girls. Great girls, but none of them were, well, me.

I began to realize I had more than just a simple crush the day I ran the full two miles up to the school over our Christmas break to see if his truck was in the parking lot for a special choir rehearsal. I remember catching a glimpse of it and suddenly feeling inexplicably upset. I'd expended all of this time and energy on this guy, yet I didn't even know if he liked me. In that moment, I was terrified that I would always be the one running, chasing, and pursuing. I worried no guy would ever deem *me* worthy of chasing.

By Valentine's Day of my senior year, I finally realized that, although I was expending all of my energy on chasing Jay, he was chasing someone else. Jay asked Taylor to prom. They were in my prom group. I sat across the table from them during dinner. Jay asked Taylor to be his girlfriend. And then Jay asked Taylor to be his wife. They are now married with a beautiful family, and I honestly could not be happier for them.

But I'm getting ahead of myself.

Just You and Me

When I started my freshman year of college at a private Christian school in west Texas, I was beyond excited. I felt like the Lord had placed the opportunity in my lap, providing me the perfect fit with intense Bible teaching and a fantastic fine arts program. Subconsciously—or maybe consciously—I had decided that when I went to college, I was going to get my degree, yes, but somewhere along the way, I was going to have a fantastic love story and then get married right after graduating. It was going to be perfect. I was going to have someone with whom to face the world! I wasn't going to have to go at it alone. I had made it through high school as a single woman (the proverbial sidekick) and wasn't anxious to repeat that phase during my college career. I recognize now that almost all of the couples from high school did not end up together in the long run, but that didn't make my current lack of a relationship any less painful for me at the time.

I really expected to find someone once I arrived at college. The year kicked off with meeting my delightful roommate. Joy was, and is, one of the most joyful people I have ever met. We had a lovely little dorm room with verses and prayer requests on our walls. We read devotions together at night after doing our daily sit-ups. Our mini fridge was filled with skim milk and cheese, and we biked everywhere we could, since neither one of us had a car. Joy had a magnetic personality, and the boys on campus were quick to notice. We were constantly being inundated with phone calls and boys stopping by on visitation days. As I said, Joy is friendly, energetic, and beautiful, and people want to be around that. But when *I* don't know someone (like the boys stopping by our room), I tend to shut down, clam up, and become the quiet friend who doesn't say anything.

I started my college career saying, "It's you and me, God! I'm totally good with this!" But the more attention the other girls on my hall received from guys, the less secure I seemed to feel. I started wondering what was wrong with me. My prayers became, "Let's make this sooner rather than later, okay? Okay. Thanks, God."

College was suddenly everything I didn't want it to be. I was a strong Christian woman who wanted to follow God, get a degree in ministry, and not need anyone but Him. I read books full of inspiration, spent time seeking the wisdom of godly advisors, and yet went to sleep terrified I was going to end up alone. It is one thing to admire the older women in ministry who never marry; it's another thing altogether to honestly desire that for your own life. So I stopped vocalizing. About every month or so, I would become fearful or desperate enough to pray about it honestly and cry out,

"Just in case You were wondering, I still want this! Please, God, I want a family of my own one day!"

That summer, as usual, I went to work as a counselor at camp. I felt uncomfortable in my own body and insecure because I wasn't attending a state college like everyone else. I saw all of these quality guy counselors and just felt as though no one would ever really like me enough to actually pursue me.

I returned from that summer of incredible work with junior high school students only to discover the crush from my freshman year was actually interested in someone else. We had barely talked over the summer, and suddenly he was totally into this gorgeous upperclassman. Too often over the years, I found myself saying, "What is wrong with me that no one else sees who I am?" I asked the question again. I was so tired of having people tell me that they couldn't wait to meet my husband. I felt defeated. "Forget meeting my husband. How about we start with a guy who wants to take me out on a date?"

That was the start of the paralyzing fear. I liked many guys and devoted my heart and thoughts to so many who didn't treat me any differently than they might any other friend. I just wanted companionship that badly. The few times I did date for more than a school dance, the relationships (obviously) ended in rejection. They did the breaking; I was the broken. Oh, and breaking is rejection. When you come from a place of receiving minimal attention from the opposite sex, rejection on top of that can leave you heartbroken. I started thinking that maybe, just maybe, if I lost some weight, *then* they would start to notice and I could finally find someone.

My whole life I had struggled with eating too much. I ate too quickly and always seemed to find room for more. I remember a routine trip to the doctor's office with my dad for a yearly checkup when I was in fourth grade. The doctor said I needed to start exercising more and eating less. Even at that point in my life, I was already hoarding. I snuck extra Oreos into the bottom of my milk glass and stashed extra snacks when I thought no one was looking. I simply loved food. The eating eventually caught up with me, and soon I couldn't exercise enough. I began to blame my lack of a love life on my weight. This caused my emotions to fluctuate frequently and wildly for years. All the while, I was deepening in my walk with the Lord. I started reading my Bible and journaling. I was learning to think of God as my Father and friend. But even on my happiest days, I still had a lingering disappointment with my body.

In the spring of my junior year, I took emotional eating to the next level. After going home for spring break and discovering that I was at my heaviest weight yet, I determined to take action. Emotional eating turned to binging and purging at a rapid pace. The desire to consume large amounts of food could be triggered by boredom, fear, or stress. I would acknowledge the feeling and then just compulsively eat.

I originally started throwing up just to feel comfortable. I was often so full that I felt sick. But it did not take long for that feeling to pass and fears about my weight to surface. Guilt would quickly set in and I would make quick plans to rid my stomach of the additional calories. Over a period of two months, I dropped a lot of weight. I was exercising six days a week, sometimes twice a day. I regulated my diet by throwing up. I was methodical. I did not want anyone to suspect anything, so I would drive to different buildings on campus to empty my stomach. I would sometimes make the decision to eat more and casually think that I would simply throw up later.

I was at the darkest time of my life, but you would never have known it on the outside. I was leading Bible studies and serving on leadership staff at my camp. I was encouraging other women to love their bodies and to see themselves in the way God had made them. Yet I continued to make myself throw up whenever I felt too full.

I did not delude myself into thinking this behavior was acceptable, godly, or healthy. I simply saw it as a means to an end. I would lose a designated amount of weight and then I would be done for good. I knew I shouldn't do it. I often prayed as I leaned over the toilet. But I was seeing results, and people were noticing the change, so I simply didn't want to stop. I even recall someone telling me that it was "great to see you taking such good care of yourself."

Strength in Weakness

> "But He said to me, 'My grace is sufficient for you, for My power is made perfect in weakness.' Therefore I will boast all the more gladly about my weaknesses, so that Christ's power may rest upon me."
> *1 Corinthians 12:9*

Since that time, the Lord has taught about His power in my weaknesses. The journey toward healing began when I realized my struggles were bigger than the strength I possessed. I purchased *Praying God's Word* by Beth Moore and found the words to describe the pit I'd been living in for months.

> A stronghold is anything that exalts itself in our minds, "pretending" to be bigger or more powerful than our God. It steals much of our focus and causes us to feel overpowered. Controlled. Mastered. Whether the stronghold is an addiction, unforgiveness toward a person who has hurt us, or despair over a loss, it is something that consumes so much of our emotional and mental energy that abundant life is strangled—our callings remain

largely unfulfilled and our believing lives are virtually ineffective.[7]

I was deeply challenged by that definition. I came to the conclusion that a stronghold was keeping me captive. I thought that I was in control of my binging and purging, but the reality was that I was being mastered by my secrets. My life was a prisoner to this destructive cycle and to the desire to receive affection from guys by any means possible. What began as a desire to drop a few pounds quickly became a battle for my freedom—a battle I was not ready to fight.

Battle Wounds

I remember when I was in fifth grade and played soccer on my school's team. We were called the Lions and proudly wore purple and gold. On one particularly sunny day, I was dressed in my uniform and standing on the sideline just waiting for my chance to play. Only I wasn't really ready. I had completely stopped paying attention. Out of nowhere, a soccer ball came flying through the air and hit me directly in the face. It was a pretty rude awakening. Not only did the ball burst the blood vessels in my left cheek, but it also raised a pretty nasty bruise in rapid time. Believe it or not, fifth-grade pictures were scheduled for the next day. True story. Pull out the yearbook and the rest of the class is all facing forward in their photos. I'm the only one with my head turned in profile.

It is easy to quickly lose sight of the fact that we are in a battle here on this earth—and that is a dangerous place to be. If we do not recognize that we are in the middle of a fight, we are vulnerable to attacks. There is no such thing as a sideline when it comes to battle. We don't get to call time-out. Think of the movie *Lord of the Rings*. I know: your favorite movie, right? If you are not familiar with the movie, just picture any big battle scene from an epic film. The soldiers are ready for war, the challenge has been given, the screaming speech has been delivered, and now the two sides are running toward each other in slow motion.

Now picture those thousands of men fighting when suddenly one of them starts daydreaming. He notices a patch of wildflowers on the ground and promptly sets down his battle-axe to gather a bouquet. *That is highly unlikely, right?*

We must keep our heads in the game! When we forget our identity as warriors in an army, we are most at risk for sustaining serious injury. Just like my soccer ball to the face scenario, I allowed my weight struggle to influence my self-esteem to such an extent that I was crippled for battle. Our enemy is not playing games. The Devil would like nothing more than to see us end up on the injured reserve list. If Satan can't take us down completely, he will do whatever he can to keep us from the field.

In the midst of my battle with an eating disorder, I was chewing on some pretty big lies that kept me from experiencing the abundant life. I convinced myself that I would feel sick if I *didn't* empty the contents of my stomach. I believed my friends, family, and coworkers would approve of me more if I lost the weight. I maintained the fear that no one really wanted to see the real me. I kept the excuses coming.

We can be really good at coming up with excuses for not surrendering our thoughts to God. Satan can provide rationalizations for *anything*. Just like I can keep hitting the snooze button in the morning and convince myself that I don't need a shower, or breakfast, or time in the Word, he can do the same with those sins we are hiding. Cutting, alcohol and drug addiction, sex, eating disorders, depression, self-loathing, lying, cheating—he has a never-ending arsenal.

I was trapped in the idea that if God was not going to give me what

I wanted, then I was going to get it my own way. I was going to do whatever it took. I was going to lose the weight, and I was going to become attractive to men.

What I didn't realize was that by doing all of this, by trying so hard to fit into the definition of beauty in our culture, I was giving up everything that made me unique and made my message authentic to young women. For almost as long as I can remember, my passion has been to help young women discover who they are in Christ. Yet I was essentially selling out to *Cosmopolitan, People* and *InStyle.*

"Nothing that sin is giving us is worth what it is taking from us."
Beth Moore[8]

I know this truth from personal experience. I bought into lies. I believed that my identity derived from others. What I really wanted was to feel loved, accepted, and desired by a guy. What I forgot in the process is that I *am* completely loved, accepted, and desired by my heavenly Father.

I began praying that God would help me change—not just for the moment but for always. It's a daily decision to make good choices about food and exercise. I have to remain in God's Word, memorize verses, and stay accountable to other women. But God is helping me fight temptation through every step of the journey.

Although I still struggle with feelings of insecurity, I've found lasting peace in my life. With support from friends and family, constant connection to the Word, and the help of a professional counselor, I am able to live freely and in victory on a regular basis. The victories began when I became active rather than passive in the process.

Fight Like You Mean It

I feel like every time I speak and share my story, people ask how I was able to resist something that was such a big temptation for me. Let's be honest: I *enjoyed* being tempted by food. I *despised* being tempted to make myself sick. But both areas of temptation led me to sin, and to feel trapped by that sin. I was living life like a hamster on a stationary wheel. I kept running and running but I wasn't getting anywhere, until one day I realized that my sin was stealing life from me. I've always wanted to live a good story and do something meaningful and exciting with my time on this earth. I also want to honor God with my life. By giving into my area of weakness—food *and* a desire to look a certain way—I let sin and its consequences write my story. Rather than honoring God, I was dishonoring Him by hurting the body He had "fearfully and wonderfully made" (Psalm 139:14).

The second half of John 10:10 is quoted by many: "I have come that they may have life, and have it to the full." I love that verse. We talked about it at length in chapter 1. I love the reminder that Jesus not only brings life to my body but He also brings me a real, meaningful, and passionate life story here and in the future that is to come.

But check out *all* of John 10:10. "The thief comes only to steal and kill and destroy; I have come that they may have life, and have it to the full."

I believe that the Devil is real, not some made-up monster from myth and legend. And I also believe that God's Word is 100 percent true. John 10:10 tells me that we have an enemy that wants to steal the very life that Jesus came to bring. Since he cannot separate us from the love of God (Romans 8:38–39), he will use anything to keep us from building and growing a relationship with our heavenly Father: busyness, anger, addiction, temptation, sin, pride, shame—you name it. He has countless ways to tempt us, *and* he fights dirty and personally.

Before we get depressed, let's remember that Jesus was also tempted. He spent forty days in the wilderness fasting and praying only to have the Devil show up when He was physically at His weakest. But Jesus didn't give in to the temptation. He fought back three times with the same weapon: the Word of God. Jesus quoted the Bible like He was wielding a sword to block off an offensive attack.

In my own story of temptation, I was only willing to admit I needed help *after* I was trapped. For so long, I thought I could just wish all my problems away. I had to recognize that I was not going to be able to break down the walls I had built on my own. I wanted to change for good, and I knew that would require the grace and power of God alone. I finally called out to God and took hold of the weapons He has given all of us. What can you do if you find yourself trapped in sin?

1. **Use your weapons.** "The weapons we fight with are not the weapons of the world. On the contrary, they have divine power to demolish strongholds. We demolish arguments and every pretension that sets itself up against the knowledge of God, and we take captive every thought to make it obedient to Christ" (2 Corinthians 10:4–5).

These powerful weapons can be found in the book of Ephesians. Paul describes in detail the armor of God. Even if you are familiar with this passage, even if you made armor out of construction paper in church as a kid, take the time to read it again! Paul talks to us about armor because we are in a battle, and it's not a game of touch football. This is a war with real weapons and real casualties.

Therefore put on the full armor of God, so that when the day
of evil comes, you may be able to stand your ground, and after
you have done everything, to stand. Stand firm then, with the
belt of truth buckled around your waist, with the breastplate of
righteousness in place, and with your feet fitted with the readiness
that comes from the gospel of peace. In addition to all this, take up
the shield of faith, with which you can extinguish all the flaming
arrows of the evil one. Take the helmet of salvation and the sword
of the Spirit, which is the word of God. And pray in the Spirit on
all occasions with all kinds of prayers and requests. With this in
mind, be alert and always keep on praying for all the saints.
Ephesians 6:13–18

My own efforts can't take down a stronghold. God is the one with the
power we need. Satan's hold comes in his ability to lie, but take that
away and he loses his power! The more we know God's Word, the
quicker we can recognize Satan's lies.

Check out the last part of the verse: "we take captive every thought to
make it obedient to Christ." That's not merely a one-time event. Notice
that the verse says "every thought." This war is not just about staying
away from lies. It is about relying on God to give us the strength and
courage to walk through each moment of every day.

2. **Prepare yourself.** Satan doesn't waste arrows where we are
    protected. If Satan knows that I have been claiming God's
    promises about comparison or how He made me, He is not
    going to waste his ammo there. Rather, he is going to focus on
    any holes in my armor. That is why it is vital to know God's
    Word like a great Samurai knows how to use his sword! You
    don't learn how to fight in the middle of a battle. You prepare
    ahead of time.

3. **Don't go at it alone.** Telling friends, a youth worker, a teacher,
    or a parent is going to make all the difference. The Devil

wants us to keep our struggles in the dark. Sharing my stronghold with someone is what initiated my long road to freedom. I had an accountability partner that walked through my recovery every step of the way. She prayed over me and handed me note cards with verses every time I saw her. She reminded me that I was not in the battle alone but had another soldier on my side, as well as the God of the universe fighting for me!

4. **Fight like you mean it.** I don't know if you've ever played basketball before, but one of the things coaches drill into your head is to get the rebound. You fight for that ball and do not give up until it is yours. God has already given us the ultimate victory through Jesus. So pray for heavenly backup and do everything on your part to fight off temptation like the warrior you are.

5. **Embrace professional help.** Professional counseling has been one of the greatest blessings in my life. Many people are willing to pay for a landscaper or personal trainer, but few of us are willing to put the care toward our emotional help. If you find yourself stuck in dangerous patterns in your thought-life or behavior, I cannot encourage you enough to seek out a counselor who can walk you through your struggles.

Our center of gravity should be God's Word. The more we are satisfied by God's love, His Word, and His presence, the more we will yearn for it. When we fill up on His Word, we carry a weapon for the offensive. King David pointed to that truth when he declared, "I have hidden your word in my heart, that I might not sin against you" (Psalm 119:11). We must learn to replace those feelings of desperation with truth from the Bible. It's not going to be an instant fix. You will still have days when you feel like the battle is too much for you, but remember the battle is not too much for the one who made you!

Victory

On most days, I proudly proclaim that I now have victory over my stronghold. And I do, at least in regards to an eating disorder. But I still have a heart disorder. Too often, I let comparison or a desire to look a certain way steal the victorious life given to me in Jesus. I don't want numbers on a scale to have control over my countenance and emotions, so each day is a battle. Every moment I choose whether I am going to seek the attention and approval of others, or if I am going to seek my Father. I have to remember that our God is completely trustworthy.

As much as I want to control *who* enters and exits my inner circle of friendships and relationships, I just can't. I'm so thankful for a God who has placed unexpected personalities in my path to shape and mold me. I'm even more thankful for the rejection (yes, the rejection) that has forced me to cling to my Father and trust His timing and provision. I have to remember how tenderly He cares for the desires of my heart, even when things don't happen the way that I expect or anticipate. When I give Him those precious desires whispered in prayer, He hears me. He is able to guard what I give Him. Paul says as much in 2 Timothy 1:12. "Yet I am not ashamed, because I know whom I have believed, and am convinced that he is able to guard what I have entrusted to him for that day."

The first time I read that verse, I tried to move on to the next verse, but my eyes pulled me back up to verse 12 again. I thought through the words Paul had chosen. "Yet I am not ashamed, because I know whom I have believed ..." Paul placed his entire trust and identity in the one in whom he believed. That belief convinced Paul that God "is able to guard what I have entrusted to him …"

Many of us believe that God has the power and ability to protect us and provide for our needs, but we seem to leave out the action verb that Paul uses: *entrust*. The dictionary defines entrust as "to give over (something) to another for care, protection, or performance."[9] Not only does Paul believe that God has the power, but he puts action to his belief. He entrusts the things burning on his heart to the Lord. Often I bring my desires and requests to the throne of God, prepared to leave them at His feet, but I find myself backing away while clutching those same requests.

If we believe that God truly does desire our good, then we should confidently and excitedly entrust our desires knowing that He will guard what we give Him. And does this act of trust happen just once? Note the end of the verse: "for that day." This is not a one-time event. This is the daily act of surrender that we will make for the rest of our lives. The benefits of daily trust will bring about peace and maturity in our lives. Some days, this will come easily, and other days, we will have to find our way back to the truth, to remember how He has promised to hear our prayers and to answer them. What a promise. What a relief. When we delight ourselves in the Lord, He cherishes the desires of our heart. Oh, that we would have the hearts to trust and take Him at His word!

"You have granted him the desire of his heart and
have not withheld the request of his lips."
Psalm 21:2

What are some of the deepest desires of your heart, the ones you might not share with anyone else? Do you trust God with those desires?

My Journal Entry

March 12, 2007

How do I as a single woman face the realities of my life and acknowledge the desires of my heart that may or may not come to fruition? Maybe I do get married and have kids and have that whole family thing. I think that sounds great. But what if that's not in His plan? What if He says no? Can I take that? Why would He say no? I want His wants to be my wants. But I find there is a big difference between wanting and living. I'm not writing this all to complain about not being married. I'm writing this because I am afraid. Yes, afraid. Afraid that I don't want what He has for me.

How can that be? I love the Lord. He is my passion, and I want to want what He wants and has. But the disappointment sneaks in, creeps in, fills in, drags down, and chokes me in my fear. I push it to the back. What kind of picture of God do I have? I don't believe that He is waiting to see if I screw things up enough on a first date to keep marriage from happening. I believe He knows my story, and He loves me.

He loves me. It brings me to tears that I cannot trust Him in this area. So what do I do? Cry every five months or so, take a deep breath, and then set out again? I think so.

Your Journal Entry

CHAPTER 5

On Guard

Above all else, guard your heart, for it is the wellspring of life.
Proverbs 4:23

Dear Twenty-Three-Year-Old Ginger,

Having someone break up with you really hurts. I know that. You know that. But don't let this pain keep you from experiencing joy in your life. Learn from the heartache, continue to guard your heart, and love others! It's okay to care; it's not okay to obsess. It's going to be all right. Just wait and see.

Love,
Today's Ginger

Heartaches

One of my favorite people and spiritual leaders is Carrie, the wife of one of my camp directors. A mother of five, she is a wealth of wisdom and knowledge. Though she would be the first to tell you she is far from perfect, you can't help but feel that her grace and humility alone give her a leg up on the rest of us. Carrie is very intentional with her words; she does not throw them around casually. Because of that, she is deliberate in her time with the young women who come to sit at her feet.

One of her favorite ways to get to know the camp's summer staff that fills her home is to ask each young woman to tell her five H's. This exercise involves each woman sharing her personal heritage, heroes, heartaches, highlights, and hopes. It's pretty straightforward yet amazing to witness.

I remember a gathering when I was with Carrie and a group of women who were sharing their heartaches. What a tear fest. I don't think I stopped crying for the entire hour we were gathered together. I tried to listen intently as the other women shared stories of divorced parents, the death of family members, and financial challenges, but my mind kept running through what my answer might possibly be.

This is going to sound awful, but in that moment, I wished that my heartache sounded more dramatic. Of course, I didn't want to actually have had something tragic happen in my life, but I didn't want to say that my heartache derived from lack of male attention. Yet even in the midst of the death of friends and family, my overarching heartache had stubbornly contained itself to one area of struggle.

I'm Single

> "Of course, the way I'm talking, it sounds like singleness is
> some horrible disease. It is not a disease. Having said that,
> however, there is something about being unintentionally single
> that can leave one feeling 'dis-eased' in a couple's world."
> *Connally Gilliam, Confessions of a Single Woman*[10]

At this point, you can quietly roll your eyes as yet another protagonist struggles with being alone.

I played the role of comic relief and sidekick to all of the great romances of middle school and high school. I desperately wanted someone to like me, and not just as friends. Yet I very much wanted to find myself content with where God had me. I wondered if I was ever going to find contentment as a single woman.

In hopes of embracing my single status, I read a few books on Christian dating and even some books on Christian non-dating. I read about putting myself out there and about how God didn't need my help in this arena. I was altogether confused, so I decided to go straight to the truth and check the Bible. I started honing in on some verses, wondering what I was supposed to do with the heart I would one day give to my dreamy husband. One in particular always stood out to me: "Above all else, guard your heart, for it is the wellspring of life" (Proverbs 4:23).

I didn't try to overthink the verse. King Solomon is giving his children advice throughout the book of Proverbs. I picture my own mom shouting out reminders as I left for school. "Don't forget your lunch! Make sure to ask your teacher about the fieldtrip! Don't talk to strangers! I love you!" All good points to remember! In this particular chapter, Solomon has been talking about living in wisdom, choosing friends that stay away from evil, and then he throws out a ton of advice right at the end. He's essentially saying, "Look straight ahead, watch where you walk, and above everything else, watch over your heart!"

I think I understand what he's saying, but we use the word *heart* to mean a lot of things. Our hearts pump blood, but they can also be broken by love. We describe full hearts, sad hearts, dear hearts, and candy hearts. I feel like shouting with Inigo Montoya from *The Princess Bride,* "You keep using that word. I do not think it means what you think it means."[11] So what is this verse actually saying about our hearts?

Solomon makes the point that Proverbs 4:23 is a very important piece of advice to remember.

"Keep vigilant watch over your heart; that's where life starts" (MSG).

"Guard your heart above all else, for it determines
the course of your life" (NLT).

The *Dake Annotated Reference Bible* goes into detail explaining this verse. By guarding our hearts, we are keeping them from going astray. The reference is "not only to the arteries which carry the blood to all parts of the body, but also to the evil and good deeds that come from the heart or the center of a man."[12]

What is clear is that in the Bible the heart is the center of the physical, mental, and spiritual life of humans. As such, the heart came to stand for the person as a whole. It is the "wellspring of life." The heart, in other words, is very important. So when you guard your heart, you guard the essence of who you are.

What is usually associated with the word *guard* or *guarding*? The president, queen, jewels, riches, prisoners, secrets, weapons, journals and diaries—I could go on. When I look at the list, I see two types of things we guard: things that are dangerous and things that are precious. Our hearts are described as wellsprings of life and as being more deceitful than anything else. I think Solomon was right on when he told his sons that hearts are worth guarding.

Hearts are precious and dangerous and have the ability to ache and break when they are wounded. But *how* do we guard them? I don't know about you, but I did not get little soldiers. I did not get a guidebook or a special talk from my teachers. I am not blaming anyone in particular; I'm just making the point that if we have failed in this area, it is generally because we did not have a game plan!

What is the number one way to guard your heart? Give it to the Lord! Give it to God, and trust that He has the best for you in the perfect time. Even after you've trusted God, there are some common sense ways to protect your heart.

> » **Keep yourself from watching movies that mess you up.** *Ever After* is my mess-up movie. It's a Cinderella story, and I absolutely lose it every time I watch Drew Barrymore's character get rescued. The movie leaves me in a heartsick state for days! Movies may not mess *you* up, but I know a lot of women who can't watch romantic comedies without feeling depressed when they end. Certain movies, books, and TV shows only serve to bring on heartache. Be strong enough to recognize when your entertainment isn't entertaining but hurting.

> » **Don't let your thoughts and hopes run past the reality of the situation.** Dreaming and talking about a future wedding is fun, but it can leave us vulnerable to unnecessary heartache. Rather than rushing ahead, we would be wise to temper our dreaming with patience!

> » **Remember that it's okay to hope for a relationship!** It's okay

to want marriage. It's okay to ask for a relationship. Keep a watch on your heart. If you are spending more time praying for and wanting "someone" than living your life by loving God, loving others, and making disciples, then ask that God would help you to desire Him more than anything else. If you are *in* a relationship and that other person has become everything to you, ask that God would also show you how He should be the greatest desire of your heart.

» **Don't be in a relationship where you have to second-guess yourself.** Be confident in who you are. If you are dating someone and feel like you have to walk on eggshells or constantly worry that you are not smart enough, funny enough, attractive enough, or whatever—it's not the relationship for you. You deserve to be cherished for who you *are,* not who you are pretending to be. Changing to conform to someone's idea of a perfect match will leave you resentful, disenchanted, and somewhere short of happily ever after.

» **Maintain friendships outside of a dating relationship.** Don't let your giddy feelings keep wisdom at bay. As an individual, you will thrive and grow when you seek the encouragement, accountability, and friendship of others. Don't take the presence of your friends for granted. Your relationship with your significant other will benefit greatly when you take time to build up your other relationships.

» **Open your hands and realize it all belongs to God.** Your relationships don't belong to you. They are a challenge, blessing, and adventure for as long as they exist. Remember your earthly relationships do not define you.

» **Don't make out with every person who takes you out on a date.** For me, adding any physicality to a relationship automatically takes my heart a step farther. For some women, that may mean eliminating kissing altogether. God is specific about protecting our hearts by telling us to protect our temples—our bodies.

» **Don't tell every guy that you love him.** Save this for the guy you marry. Let's face it: we want to be in love. But don't rush it! Song of Solomon—there's that wise guy again!—has some great advice about being patient when it comes to love. "Don't excite love, don't stir it up, until the time is ripe and you're ready" (Song of Solomon 2:7 MSG). When dating relationships come, **take the slow road. It's worth it.**

» **Establish relational lifeboats.** By setting boundaries in our relationships, we make sure we don't end up sinking in the Pacific Ocean. Remember the story of the *Titanic?* It was a beautiful ship of dreams. Deemed unsinkable by the architects and press, the *Titanic* was set for a maiden voyage from Ireland to New York. As you know, the ship collided with an iceberg and 1,516 people perished at sea. The iceberg was not the ultimate cause of these deaths—it was the shortage of lifeboats. Had there been enough lifeboats for all of the crew and passengers present, there would likely have been enough time to save every life.

Don't place yourself in situations that don't have lifeboats. Know your weaknesses. Several couples I know have found success by making these permanent lifeboats: Don't lie down on a couch together. Don't be alone together. Make sure someone knows your selected curfew rather than having an open-ended evening. And don't remove any clothing.

Here's the deal: the longer you are in a relationship (dating or engaged), the more you want to be together and experience intimacy together.

That's normal, so be prepared. Don't have a *Titanic* moment and increase your speed if you don't have lifeboats in place.

> » **Remain sexually abstinent.** Saving yourself for marriage isn't just an overly conservative idea held by your parents and your youth pastor. It's one of God's commands and one of the best ways to guard your heart. Check out Paul's thoughts in 1 Thessalonians 4:3–8 in the God's Word translation.
>
> It is God's will that you keep away from sexual sin as a mark of your devotion to Him. Each of you should know that finding a husband or wife for yourself is to be done in a holy and honorable way, not in the passionate, lustful way of people who don't know God. No one should take advantage of or exploit other believers that way. The Lord is the one who punishes people for all these things. We've already told you and warned you about this. God didn't call us to be sexually immoral but to be holy. Therefore, whoever rejects this order is not rejecting human authority but God, who gives you his Holy Spirit.

I once heard a speaker compare this passage to protecting your cheesecake. Imagine that you've gone to a restaurant and ordered an amazing meal *and* dessert, but you are too full to eat your dessert— your cheesecake. You have the waiter box up your cheesecake and you carry it safely home on your lap. Once you get home, you go to extreme lengths to protect the cheesecake—or at least I do. The problem with the Styrofoam box is that it can allow odors from other foods to enter, so you wrap your boxed cheesecake in foil. And just to make sure that none of your family members decide to accidentally eat your cheesecake, you write your name all over that foil. "GINGER's

CHEESECAKE: KEEP OUT!" You mark the date, and for good measure, you add a threat. "This cheesecake has been poisoned. Do not eat or you will die." Then you find the sturdiest shelf and place your dessert goodness all the way at the back and hide it behind a row of milk, cranberry juice, and chocolate syrup. Ain't nobody gonna mess with your cheesecake.

Honoring God with our modesty and sexuality is something that we should take seriously. Paul reminds us that when we sin against our body, we don't just hurt ourselves but we sin against God—a God who has called us to be set apart and holy. Aren't you more valuable than *cheesecake*?

If you're up for it, let's pause for a little "guard your heart" true-or-false quiz. Ready?

True or False

I can wear whatever I want, as long as it looks cute.

                                           T   F

Sending pictures of myself with minimal or no clothing via text is no big deal.

                                           T   F

If I go out with a guy, I owe him something—at least a kiss.

                                           T   F

As long as I love the guy, having sex is the next step in the relationship.

                                           T   F

Let's talk through each of these and see if we can get a clue to the answers from a biblical perspective.

I can wear whatever I want, as long as it looks cute.

I get the argument. You like the bikini/skirt/top/dress. You like how you look and it's comfortable. What's the big deal? If a guy wants to keep his eyes pure, that is his job, not mine. Let's check 1 Thessalonians 4 again, but this time in the New International Version.

> It is God's will that you should be sanctified: that you should avoid sexual immorality; that each of you should learn to control your own body in a way that is holy and honorable, not in passionate lust like the pagans, who do not know God; and that *in this matter no one should wrong or take advantage of a brother or sister.*
> 1 Thessalonians 4:3-8 (emphasis added)

When you dress modestly, you guard the hearts of our brothers. And as we've established before, guarding hearts is important work. Guys are visually driven—that's not a shocking statement. You can say you are dressing for yourself or your friends all you want, but the responsibility to guard hearts and eyes is still partially yours. A good starting place is to make sure the three B's are covered: boobs, bottom, and belly. Walking around your house in a tube top is cool. Going to dinner with a group of your friends when your bottom is hanging out of your shorts is not cool. The type of bait you use will determine the fish you will catch. Are you looking for a guy who is in the relationship because of your heart? Give him a chance to see your heart rather than your cleavage. This is not a rulebook to make you look or act like a prude. The way we behave, dress, and communicate with the opposite sex should demonstrate discretion rather than indiscretion. The goal is to live in modesty, and the truth is that modesty is more than the length of your shorts. It is a mind-set.

Sending pictures of myself with minimal or no clothing via text is no big deal.

False times a zillion. When you send pictures of yourself, you are essentially sending that image to the entire world. While you may trust the fellow who requested that photo, I certainly don't. Don't believe me? The National Campaign to Prevent Teen and Unplanned Pregnancy and CosmoGirl.com recently conducted a survey asking teens if they are sending or posting sexually suggestive messages. The results?

> According to a survey of American adolescents, three out of four think sharing personal information or photos online falls between "somewhat safe" and "somewhat unsafe," similar to how they perceive the dangers of underage drinking.

> Where teens fall short is in their understanding of the legal ramifications of sexting. Simply stated, sending sexts of people under 18 years of age is illegal. Beyond online reputation, teens who send sexually explicit photos can be convicted of child pornography charges and have their names permanently placed on registered sex offender lists. One Florida youth received five years of probation and registration as a sex offender when he sent nude photos of his ex-girlfriend to her entire family and school.

> This scenario is made worse by the fact that teens are highly likely to share the sexts they receive, with little regard to the electronic privacy of the sender. Even if your child would never engage in sexting under normal circumstances, the temptation to

forward unsolicited naked photos of a classmate ...
can be hard to resist. But it can land your child in
jail.

Reputation.com[13]

So forget the idea that this is just between you and the cute boy from
history class. This isn't the kind of attention you want. The images
you text, video message, or even post on Instagram *permanently* exist.
They cannot be erased.

If I go out with a guy, I owe him something—at least a kiss.

So a guy takes you out. Maybe he picks you up, or maybe he
meets you at the movies. He drops twenty dollars on a movie and
another twenty dollars on snacks. He reaches over to hold your
hand during the movie. Maybe that's cool with you, and maybe
you feel like you owe him. After all, he did just pay forty dollars
to spend some time with you. Perhaps when it comes to saying
good-bye, you are really hoping he doesn't try to kiss you yet;
maybe you just aren't ready. But then he brings up the movie, so
you oblige.

Girlfriend, you owe that boy nothing more than to be polite. How
does this translate on your date? If he reaches for your hand but you
aren't feeling it, just say, "No, thank you." If he points out the forty
dollars he spent on you and expects a kiss, simply reply, "I am so
appreciative, but I am just not ready to kiss."

If you think this is silly, let me just remind you that this guy just spent
the evening with a daughter of the King of Kings! Read my words:
you don't owe him anything—not sex, not a kiss, not a hug, not even a

fist bump if you feel uncomfortable. You were bought at a price; don't give that up for a night at the movies.

As long as I love the guy, having sex is the next step in the relationship.

Remember the cheesecake story? God says that sex is an amazing gift, but it is a gift for marriage. Here is how Paul explains in 1 Corinthians 6:16–20 (MSG, emphasis added).

> There's more to sex than mere skin on skin. Sex is as much spiritual mystery as physical fact. As written in Scripture, "The two become one." Since we want to become spiritually one with the Master, *we must not pursue the kind of sex that avoids commitment and intimacy, leaving us more lonely than ever—the kind of sex that can never "become one."* There is a sense in which sexual sins are different from all others. In sexual sin we violate the sacredness of our own bodies, these bodies that were made for God-given and God-modeled love, for "becoming one" with another. Or didn't you realize that your body is a sacred place, the place of the Holy Spirit? Don't you see that you can't live however you please, squandering what God paid such a high price for? The physical part of you is not some piece of property belonging to the spiritual part of you. God owns the whole works. So let people see God in and through your body.

Our sexuality is a big deal to God. He repeatedly talks about guarding our hearts by protecting our bodies. If your desire is to be a woman who is known for her character rather than her figure, then think ahead. The goal is not to make you guilt-ridden about the past or worried about your future. It is to remind you that we all *thrive* with boundaries. The boundaries are set because He loves us and He wants to protect our hearts.

Each of has an area of struggle, and yours may very well involve sex. If these verses and paragraphs have left you feeling shamed in any way, I want to stop for a moment and remind you of the good news. God has loved each of us at our lowest and weakest moments. Romans 5:6 in the New Living Translation says, "When we were utterly helpless, Christ came at just the right time and died for us sinners."

God does not wait for us to pull it together. He reached out and sent His son, Jesus, when *we were utterly helpless.* I like to picture a two-year-old who has just thrown up and made a huge mess. A loving father doesn't look at the kid and yell, "You'd better clean that up!" Instead, the parent picks up the frightened and dirty child, hugs, and then cleans them. This is good news for all of us, for we have all missed the mark of perfection. Whether an eating disorder, lying, cheating, or sexual regrets—the promise of grace is for everyone who receives it. "Yet to all who did receive him, to those who believed in his name, he gave the right to become children of God" (John 1:12).

When we choose to make guilt and shame our daily companions, we are not accepting the gift of God. There is a good kind of guilt that leads to repentance, but if you find yourself full of fear rather than peace, chances are that grace is a vocabulary word and not a reality for you. I know. I spent far too many years overcome with the shame of my own mistakes. The big message of God's love should give us real hope for each day.

"Are you tired? Worn out? Burned out on religion? Come to me. Get away with me and you'll recover your life. I'll show you how to take a real rest. Walk with me and work with me—watch how I do it. Learn the unforced rhythms of grace. I won't lay anything heavy or ill-fitting on you. Keep company with me and you'll learn to live freely and lightly."
Matthew 11:28–30 (MSG)

The Extreme

"To love at all is to be vulnerable. Love anything, and your heart will certainly be wrung and possibly broken. If you want to make sure of keeping it intact, you must give your heart to no one, not even to an animal. Wrap it carefully round with hobbies and little luxuries; avoid all entanglements; lock it up safe in the casket or coffin of your selfishness. But in that casket—safe, dark, motionless, airless—it will change. It will not be broken; it will become unbreakable, impenetrable, and irredeemable."
C. S. Lewis, The Four Loves[14]

Sometimes, I wish Solomon had something to say about the other side of dating, like, "How do I put myself out there?"

After my heart was shattered a few times, I began to take guarding to the extreme. I decided enough was enough. I was not going to do any more grieving, and I took it too far. I became a giant block of ice. When asked about my opinions or feelings, I would change the topic, shy away from sharing, and refrain from making eye contact with the opposite sex. We won't go into my superstar dating history, but I will say that I have had my fair share of being on the "broken" side of the breakup. I've had fewer relationships than I have fingers—on my right hand. Get the picture? By the time I was actually *in* a relationship, I lived in terror that I was going to *lose* the relationship. But I didn't want to be that way! I was a strong, independent woman who had Jesus as her Bridegroom. I didn't *need* anyone, right?

One breakup in particular pointed out how little I trusted God's plan. The guy informed me that God wasn't giving our relationship the green light. This was nothing new; God had done this in two previous relationships. I said I trusted God, so I couldn't fault the guy. Yet I was overcome with painful dread. My eyes filled with tears as I realized that, once again, I would be alone. It hurt to be rejected, but more than that, it hurt to realize how much I dreaded being single. I took precautions to guard my heart and I soaked up God's truth, so why was I so terrified of being alone?

The truth is I thought being alone made me stronger. Somehow, I believed that I wouldn't get to have someone until I learned how to be alone. I do know that loneliness can be a tool used to draw us closer to God, and that there are times in our lives when we will have different forms of community, but I do not think that loneliness is next to godliness. At least I do not believe that anymore.

In the first two chapters of Genesis, God creates the world and declares everything He has created to be good, and the creation of Adam is described as *very* good. But in Genesis 2, we come across one hiccup. God places Adam in the garden of Eden and says, "It is not good for the man to be alone. I will make a helper suitable for him" (Genesis 2:18). God and Adam search the garden and go through every animal to find the perfect helper. Eventually, we see that none is found. God even says no to the dog and the cat! God then creates Eve.

Remember that it's not just animal companionship for Adam, *but a partner*. The desire for a companion is not wrong. The fact that we want to feel loved, protected, or comforted is not sin, nor is it weakness. The danger comes when we make any other person our fulfillment.

Being lonely is not the original intention. In fact, it's *not good*. That's why we need community; we need each other. Yes, there are seasons when we will have fewer friends than other times. When I first moved to Arizona, I was starving for friendship with young, single women my own age. God was gracious to provide me two single girlfriends for a period of time, and then they both got married. (Of course, I handled it really well. "Woe is me, *yadda, yadda* … Lord, help!")

I should not have been beating myself up for wanting to be in a relationship. If God had wanted this life to just be about *Adam and God*, He wouldn't have added Eve into the equation. Relationships have been deemed good, and marriage most definitely pleases God, but total dependency on another human rather than God? That is idolatry. Community is good. Loneliness is not good. Idolatry is very bad. His words, not mine. 1 John 5:21 says, "Dear children, keep yourselves from idols." People are some of the easiest things to worship other than God.

I am the first to admit that I don't want my heart to run away with me, but at the same time, I can close myself off in relationships. Several kind gentlemen have told me that if I didn't share how I was feeling, then they didn't have the ability to lead our relationship. We don't just get to hang around like a dartboard and hope that one day *the* guy is just going to throw the dart that hits the bull's-eye. It takes work from both parties.

I have a go-to friend when it comes to relationships. She's given me countless words of wisdom over the years, and her most frequent comment actually comes from her dad. Megan is quick to remind me that if I want to win big, I have to be willing to risk big.

This may come as a shock to you, but men are not mind readers. I know. This would have been good to know from the beginning, right? I have sent hundreds of hints toward prospective guys only to find myself saying, *"Why isn't he doing anything?"* Sometimes, they need more than a hint.

» **Be specific.** Only show one guy partiality at a time.

» **Be intentional.** Ask him about his life and interests; convey that you want to get to know him. Remember the things he tells you.

» **Be engaging.** Rather than playing it super cool or hard to get, try smiling when you see him!

I still believe that the relationship needs to start with the guy, so I'm not suggesting you just start asking them out. And while I admittedly don't have all the answers, I do think it comes down to a balance of protecting what God has given us *while* being willing to risk rejection. Continue to filter your emotions through the truth of God's Word. Be real with yourself and with your trusted friends. Be open and honest in prayer. Keep your situation in perspective, and realize if a romantic relationship truly is to be part of your story, the master storyteller knows *exactly* how and when to bring the characters together.

I was talking to a young woman who posed this question to me: what do you do when you feel like you don't want to give even a part of your heart away if it's not to your husband?

I challenged her with the fact that I have given parts of my heart away my entire life—and I'm not even referring to dating relationships. Just because we guard our hearts doesn't mean that we wall them off and cover them in barbed wire. Instead, guarding our hearts should always be accompanied with *wisdom*. When we guard, we carefully choose how and when we will share of our hearts. My friends hold a part of my heart. I give of myself when I love my parents and my family. But by opening my heart to them, I am risking the possibility of disappointment and pain. The reason those relationships can hurt the most is because we have invested so much of our hearts in those people we love most. In the end, I think the benefits far outweigh the risk.

Relationships are worth the investment. Trust and believe that God has things under control and that your life doesn't surprise Him! He knows your worries before you express them. Find freedom in placing the desires of your heart with the one who created your heart.

Good Gifts

Trusting God with the desires of your heart is a huge step in learning to love. Believe that He cares far more for your heart than you do. If He really *is* the expert, He will give you exactly what you need in the perfect timing. God isn't waiting to pull back the curtain and exclaim, "Ha! Sucker! Now you'll be single forever! Now you'll never get what you want!"

Remember we serve a God who loves to give good gifts to His children.

> "If your child asks you for bread, would any of you give him
> a stone? Or if your child asks for a fish, would you give him a
> snake? Even though you're evil, you know how to give good
> gifts to your children. So how much more will your Father
> in heaven give good things to those who ask Him?"
> *Matthew 7:9–11 (GW)*

Part of my heart issues stemmed from the fear of rejection. No one likes to be rejected. But relationships with the opposite sex end in one of two ways: rejection or marriage. An amazing little book on this topic that offered a total paradigm shift for me is *The Art of Rejection* by Haley and Michael DiMarco. They reminded me that rejection can be a good thing. Change is hard and rejection doesn't *feel* good, but it helps us to weed out relationships that either aren't in our best interests or simply aren't meant to end in marriage. I would not be where I am today if rejection hadn't come into play. I would have missed out on my own adventure out in the desert. Rejection made the choice for me.

> "Yes, you are good enough, but you aren't for them. Those are two different issues. Your goodness has nothing to do with them. You are two different people with two different lives that happened to cross. Just because this person has rejected you doesn't mean you are defective or bad."
> *Haley and Michael DiMarco, The Art of Rejection*[15]

In order to win big in relationships, I have to be willing to risk. I have to be willing to love others. Wisdom simply reminds us to proceed with caution! Remember the big commands? Love God. Love others. Straight up, that's what the Father asked of us.

There was a big movement when I was in high school in the late '90s to refrain from dating altogether. It may have seemed like I was kissing dating good-bye, but the truth is I certainly *would* have been dating in college if anyone came asking.

I'm not saying it's a bad thing to ward off men for a while, especially if you're waiting for the right kind of guy. Yes, he is worth waiting for! But it doesn't mean that you are any holier for *not* dating. It all comes back to the heart. My heart can be just as selfish sitting at home on a Friday night and reading Christian fiction as it can be on a date at the Olive Garden.

I believe that it is imperative for you to reach a point where you can identify what is going on in your heart and in your mind. Like any good soldier, you have to know your strong points and your weak points. Run your thoughts through God's filter. Check your thoughts with truth. Spend time in God's Word and let Him remind you how He alone can fill the yearnings of your heart.

> "Whom have I in heaven but you? And earth has nothing I desire besides you. My flesh and my heart may fail, but God is the strength of my heart and my portion forever."
> *Psalm 73:25–26*

That verse became my battle cry, rather than my former declaration that singleness was next to godliness.

Whether we are single or taken, struggling physically or earning a badge in saving sex for marriage, what honors God most is when we give Him our hearts. There is nothing you have done, no mistakes you have made, or any lies you have believed that can keep you from the love of your maker. Remember that He desires to give us *good* gifts! May we learn to hope in His promises, trust His timing, and join in the tender protection of our hearts.

> "But the eyes of the LORD are on those who fear him, on those whose hope is in his unfailing love, to deliver them from death and keep them alive in famine. We wait in hope for the LORD; he is our help and our shield. In him our hearts rejoice, for we trust in his holy name. May your unfailing love rest upon us, O LORD, even as we put our hope in you."
> *Psalm 33:18–20*

Do you believe that your heart is worth protecting?
How are you currently treating your heart?

My Journal Entries

June 5, 2005

Father, You are the only one who can ever truly fill me or assure me with Your constant affirmation. Today I am entrusting You with my heart and his. I need you to guard what I have entrusted you with! Your Word says, "Yet I am not ashamed because I know whom I have believed and am convinced that He is able to guard what I have entrusted to Him for that day" (2 Timothy 1:12). I entrust my heart and this relationship to you. I let go. If this is not the one for me, do your thing. I trust you.

June 6, 2005

Well. That's it. The relationship is over. Thank You, Lord, for the immediate comfort of friends. Somehow, use this in my life for Your glory. I am Yours—wholly Yours.

Father, You are faithful to answer my prayers as I call, and I thank You for that. I praise You that You are sovereign in my life and You know what is best for me. I can't explain You, but thank You for guarding my heart.

Your Journal Entry

CHAPTER 6

Trust the Expert

Trust in the LORD with all your heart and lean not on
your own understanding; in all your ways acknowledge
him, and he will make your paths straight.
Proverbs 3:5–6

Dear Twenty-Five-Year-Old Ginger,

I know that what you really want is to have someone. It's okay.
God said it's not good for us to be alone. You don't have to do
any of this alone; look at the loving people around you! Trust
your Father. It's just like we thought. His timing works out for
the best.

Love,
Today's Ginger

Great Expectations

A wise friend is always quick to remind me that *when expectations and reality don't meet up, all that's left is disappointment.*

It's amazing how much truth is found in that simple statement. My happiness on any given day can greatly be affected by unmet expectations. Birthdays are the worst. I cannot tell you how many birthdays go down as least favorite days in my life.

The night before my twenty-eighth birthday, I took special pains to lower my expectations and prepare myself. No one wants to enter the day hoping for a surprise party and end up crying in a bathtub at 11:00 p.m. while listening to Josh Groban. (Trust me: I know.) I told myself to expect no gifts to arrive, no one at the office to remember, and nothing special or out of the ordinary. Thankfully, it was by far one of the best birthdays to date!

Lowering expectations can allow for pleasant surprises, but it can also deplete the ability to dream or even hope for great things. I am starting to wonder if all expectations derive from selfish motivations or if I need to look at the entire idea in a different light. Rather than allowing my mood to be dictated by the hoped-for actions of others, I must ground my hope in something more stable than the human condition. I cannot demand that the entire world reads my mind and behaves in the manner I deem acceptable. That is just not going to work.

Recommendations of the Chef

During my sophomore year in college, I spent a semester studying in England. When it came time to plan spring break, I had one destination on my mind: Italy. I made plans with my friend Katie for the perfect trip roaming around the Italian countryside. We met in Milan and traveled to Florence, Fiesole, and Venice. We spent hours riding trains, walking in museums, and trying to understand the menus at sidewalk cafes. It was an experience full of terrifying and transcendent moments for two twenty-year-olds trying to act like adults.

On our last evening in Venice, after spending an hour on a gondola ride with a driver who sang only a medley of Beatles classics, we decided to eat a meal to rival Italy itself. Katie's grandfather had given us one hundred euros with specific instructions that it be spent on one fantastic Italian meal during our trip. We asked several locals for suggestions and ended up at Antica Trattoria PosteVecie, one of the oldest restaurants in Venice. It was to be our final meal before returning to the significantly less fabulous fare offered to us by the United Kingdom. (Sorry, but who puts cottage cheese on a hamburger?)

We made our way to the banquet table in the dimly lit establishment. Our waitress approached and we gave her our only request. "Bring us whatever the chef recommends. We have one hundred euros and we are spending it all tonight."

Five courses and two full stomachs later, we determined that Katie's grandfather was the greatest person to have ever walked the earth. Italy had offered us extraordinary cuisine before, but this was an entirely new level of fine dining. In retrospect, I realize that our meal would have been amazing even if we had only had fifty euros. What made our meal so fabulous were the expert selections of our Italian chef.

It's a simple concept but one I often forget. I tend to assume that my decisions will make for the most memorable meal. But without the thoughts of an expert, my Italian feast could have ended up like an appetizer from the Olive Garden. Although I'm fine with the Olive Garden, it just can't compete with Trattoria PosteVecie.

The chef knows. He knows what pairs well together and what can make an ordinary dinner completely extravagant and delightful. I like to think I'm the expert when it comes to what I need in my life. If there's one thing I want to get right, it's my life! I have list after list of things to do before I die. I would probably order all the courses of my life from a menu if it were an option. It seems I want God to sign off on my dreams without even asking for His recommendations.

I had a mentor who once challenged a room full of young women to make a list of the dreams and hopes we had for our lives—a bucket list, if you will. It was a really cool exercise, so I want to give you the opportunity to try it. I want you to just start writing down some of the dreams you have for your life. Maybe you express some of them all the time, or maybe some of them are secrets you keep to yourself. I want you to take three to five minutes and jot down a few things.

Need some starters? Here are a few from my list: travel to Africa, sail around Greece, finish my master's degree, write a book (woohoo!), learn to play the drums, plant a flower garden, have a family, attend an opera, and take a medical missions trip. Now it's your turn to make a list in the space provided. *Have at it!*

Bucket List

How did it go for you? When I did the exercise, five minutes came and went and I could clearly tell that I had the most items on my list. I love lists. I love dreaming. I'm also very competitive. I found myself shouting (on the inside), "I am so amazing at this!"

I waited in expectation for our mentor to have us call out the number of items on our list. I was ready to win. But then she totally turned things upside down when she said, "How does your list look? Good? Dreams are amazing. They help us to live with hope and to set goals. But too often, we can treat God like our short-order cook. We order eggs and ask for them sunny-side up. When they come out as an omelet, we want to send them back! God is our creator and the author of our lives. He is the expert. *So, why don't we trust Him?* Are you taking your list, waving it at God, and then asking Him to sign off on your order?"

We were then encouraged to turn the paper over and to simply sign the blank side. What an initially terrifying thought. I don't get to make my own list? What if He fills my blank sheet with singleness, a boring job, loneliness, sickness, disappointment, and lots of other challenging things?

If I ask the chef for the house special, he's not going to bring me bologna and mayonnaise (sick). The chef can be counted on to bring me *good* things! Why was I so terrified of what the Lord might have for my life? I was unknowingly hanging all of my hopes on that list and I hadn't once bothered to ask the expert or really trust what He might have for me.

Everything Changes

I've always loved Christmas Eve. I love the anticipation of the season, the candles in the church service, and the expectation of Christmas morning. As a child, it was almost impossible to fall asleep on

Christmas Eve. I tried counting sheep, watching the rotations of the fan blades, clearing my mind, and praying, but it still felt like I was up half the night! I'm not very good at waiting.

The church season prior to Christmas is called Advent, meaning arrival or coming. It's a way to remind us to prepare our hearts for the coming of Jesus. While Advent only lasts about five weeks for us, it kept the Israelites waiting forty-two generations! In Genesis 3, God first promises a Messiah who would come to defeat death. And so they waited through Abraham, Isaac, Jacob, Joseph, Moses, Boaz, Obed, Jesse, David, Solomon, Isaiah, Jeremiah, and Micah, and then finally in the first book of the New Testament we read, "This is how the birth of Jesus Christ came about: His mother Mary was pledged to be married to Joseph, but before they came together, she was found to be with child through the Holy Spirit" (Matthew 1:18).

When I read the gospels, I usually skim through the Christmas story. The nativity is repeated so often during December that I consider my Christmas story quota filled. But recently I started researching Mary, the mother of Jesus, and discovered something both deeply humbling and encouraging.

Did you know that Jewish engagements at this time actually looked a lot different from what you know about modern engagements? The father of the groom more than likely made the choice of the bride for his son. The groom paid a dowry to the father of the bride. Initially, a contract was made with a ceremony that bound the man and woman together as a married couple, but it wasn't the wedding ceremony. This agreement was so binding that it could only be broken by a divorce. The two were considered husband and wife but would spend the entire next year living apart and most certainly not sharing a bed.

During this yearlong engagement, the husband would be building an addition to his parents' house. Once completed, this room would be the home for his new bride. A rabbi would inspect the home, and it would not be considered completed until it was deemed an improvement over where the bride was currently living. Once the father of the groom gave the go-ahead, the groom would gather his wedding party and begin the walk to retrieve his bride. The bride would have spent the last year purifying herself, sewing her wedding clothes, and preparing for marriage.

And now it was Mary's chance to be the bride. She was pledged to be married to Joseph. She was preparing herself for the wedding and the marriage. She had seen countless girls from her village make their own journey with their husbands, and now it was her turn. It *was* until the day everything changed.

> "In the sixth month, God sent the angel Gabriel to Nazareth, a town in Galilee, to a virgin pledged to be married to a man named Joseph, a descendant of David. The virgin's name was Mary. The angel went to her and said, 'Greetings, you who are highly favored! The Lord is with you.'"
> *Luke 1:26–28*

An angel approached a teenage village girl and pronounced her to be favored by God and to have the presence of God with her! Was Mary a saint from the start?

We know from Scripture that God places a high value on the humble and the pure in heart. James 4:8 states, "Come near to God and God will come near to you."

Mary was not any more perfect than Eve or King David. She was not sinless. In fact, she calls the Messiah "My Savior" in Luke 1:47. Mary recognized that she was indeed a sinner in need of a Savior.

But Mary shows us that before God called her to this role, she had filled up on Him. She knew her God.

With school, work, friendships, and thinking about college and the future, it's really easy to focus on anything *but* our relationship with God. God desires your heart much more than anything. A very incredible woman in my life once said, "It is better to be anything-deprived rather than God-deprived." This means that sometimes we sacrifice sleep, hanging out with friends, or going shopping in order to fill up on the good stuff: God's Word and spending time in His presence. Remember: don't fill up on the chips and salsa and forget to leave room for your meal!

I believe that Mary had been filling up on the good stuff. How can I know that? Just check out her response to the fact that she, a virgin, was going to have a baby. And not just any baby, mind you. She was going to birth the Savior of the world! Mary had been preparing her heart for this her entire life.

> Mary was greatly troubled at his words and wondered what kind of greeting this might be. But the angel said to her, "Do not be afraid, Mary, you have found favor with God. You will be with child and give birth to a son, and you are to give him the name Jesus. He will be great and will be called the Son of the Most High. The Lord God will give him the throne of his father David, and he will reign over the house of Jacob forever; his kingdom will never end."

> "How will this be," Mary asked the angel, "since I am a virgin?" The angel answered, "The Holy Spirit will come upon you and the power of the Most High will overshadow you. So the holy one to be born will be called the Son of God. Even Elizabeth your relative is going to have a child in her old age, and she who was said to be barren

is in her sixth month. For nothing is impossible with God."

"I am the Lord's servant," Mary answered. "May it be to me as you have said."

Luke 1:29–38

What do you think those first few moments were like for Mary after the angel left? I do not think she exclaimed, "Yes! *Virgin Mary.* I am totally digging the new name!" I imagine it went something more like this:

Was I dreaming?

Oh, God. Have You really called me for this? I know, as the angel said, that nothing is impossible with You. But carrying the Messiah? I still can't believe it. What an ordinary start to the day. And now, my goodness. I have to sit down. No, I can't sit down.

Mary, calm down. Deep breaths. I'm going to have a baby. I'm going to have a baby. Am I with child now? Could the Messiah we've longed for, hoped for, prayed for be here now—with me?

I'm no one. I'm just an ordinary girl planning her wedding. My wedding! Abba Father, what of Joseph? What of our plans? What of our life together? Would he ever want me like this? Will he ever believe me? What a conversation. I can just imagine it.

"Hello, my love. I need to tell you something— something that will be hard for you to understand

and even harder for you to believe. I'm pregnant, but I have not been unfaithful to you."

"Of course. And whose child is it?" he'll ask.

"Abba Father's."

"The heavenly Father's?" he'll question.

"I am carrying the Messiah."

"Well, that makes sense. Can I get you anything?" he'll say, and then everything will be as it was.

Or will it?

No. No. No. This isn't how this is supposed to go. He was preparing our home for us. He was making it ready. My dowry had been paid. I was just waiting for him to come and get me. And now he won't want me. No one will. No one will.

Not even my parents. My father. My mother. Oh, God. Help me. I can hide it for a while, but even still, when Joseph finds out, he will come to my father and demand—he could have me killed! He could have me stoned. But he wouldn't, would he? How will any of them believe me? They will all be mocked because of me.

Oh, but Abba, I am thankful. Thank You for choosing me. May it be to me as You have said. The angel. Me, highly favored? How? How did You choose me? The line of David, and he will rule over the house of Jacob forever. Am I royalty? And the name Jesus—so

ordinary. There are three in Nazareth with the name
that are not even walking. Why give this king the
name Jesus? Why not something strong like James
or Mark? Why?

I'm sorry for the questions. It's just not what I expected.
Everything is going to change because of this. Because
of You. Oh, heaven, give me strength for this task. I
am feeble and prone to doubt. But I am Your servant.
May it be to me as You have declared, Lord.

I may shake in fear. I may doubt. But You, Lord,
stand firm just as You have done with Abraham,
Isaac, Jacob, and Judah.

Deep breaths.

I give up. I will not look back and wish it had been
what I wanted. I will put all of my hope in You. I will
not fear though the earth gives way.

Perhaps I'm way off, but Mary's initial response to the angel leads me
to believe that she trusted God's best for her. "I am the Lord's servant;
may it be to me as you have said" (Luke 1:38).

In every translation of Luke, Mary still says, "I'm Yours, God. I will
take whatever You want to give me, even if it's hard." Mary had
devoted herself to the Lord to the point that she trusted His judgment
above all else. Look what she was willing to offer up to God: wedding
plans, her wedding dress, her reputation and standing, emotional
stability, friends, others' assumptions, and naming her child. Matthew
1:19 tells us that Joseph was going to divorce her privately, but the
truth is that she could have been exposed to public shame and even
death (Deuteronomy 22:25–28).

Mary actively places her expectation on God, just like the psalmist. "My soul, wait silently for God alone, for my expectation is from Him" (Psalm 62:5, NKJV).

More than just accepting the news of the angel, Mary shows a remarkably thankful spirit when she goes to visit her cousin Elizabeth. Whether she was sent by her family to avoid rumors or because she simply wanted someone to celebrate with, she goes to see her cousin who has also had an encounter with the Lord and the gift of a son. As Mary approaches, the baby in Elizabeth's womb leaps for joy. Elizabeth exclaims that Mary is blessed to carry the Lord and blessed to believe that what God had said *would* be accomplished.

In the midst of unlikely, uncomfortable, and life-altering news, Mary's response to the Savior is one of *gratitude*. Look at the words that pour forth from her heart in Luke 1:46–56.

> My soul doth magnify the Lord and my spirit doth rejoice in God my Savior.
>
> For He has been mindful of the humble state of His servant.
>
> From now on all generations will call me blessed,
>
> For the Mighty One has done great things for me— Holy is His name.
>
> His mercy extends to those who fear Him, from generation to generation.
>
> He has performed mighty deeds with His arm;
>
> He has scattered those who are proud in their innermost thoughts.

He has brought down rulers from their thrones

But has lifted up the humble.

He has filled the hungry with good things

But has sent the rich away empty.

He has helped His servant Israel, remembering to
be merciful

To Abraham and His descendants forever,

Even as He said to our fathers.

Everything she had planned for her life at that point changed in one instant. I don't think Mary ever returned to normal, naïve, innocent Mary. She probably saw the worst in people after her pregnancy became obvious. It all changed: dreams, plans, and hopes. She must have felt fairly apprehensive about what was asked of her. Like most girls, she had probably been dreaming about her wedding day, and it didn't include being pregnant. When she envisioned the birth of her first child, she probably didn't picture a barn. But all of that paled in comparison as she loved and cared for the Messiah within her. Mary chose not to look back but to lean forward while trusting in her heavenly Father.

Mary reminds us to live expectantly trusting our Father—the one who makes good on all His promises. In Mary we see a willingness to open her hands, listen to God's call, and trust His dreams for her, rather than clinging to her own.

The Ram

I fell for a wonderful guy—couldn't believe God's timing and provision—only to have him break up with me one week later. I committed to move to Africa. I packed my stuff into storage, paid for shots, and set my mind and heart where I felt God was calling me, only to have my application turned down. I took on the new, exciting, and scary position at work only to have my boss resign the day I started. I turned down a job back home in Texas only to find myself desperately wanting the opportunity to change my answer one month later.

Have you ever found yourself in a similar situation?

I have wanted to follow God with all my heart, mind, and strength for as long as I can remember. I offered up my career, and my idea of home and family, and told Him that if He led, I would follow. I don't know if I ever bargained on following Him when I did not have reassurance about what was coming next.

The perfect example of someone who demonstrates obedience in the midst of unknowns is a man named Abraham.

Abraham is widely recognized as the father of the Israelite nation, but he did not start out that way. Abraham heard God's call and moved from the country of Ur and into the land of promise. Land wasn't the only part of God's promise. Abraham firmly believed God's promise that as senior citizens, he and his barren wife, Sarah, would see their family tree expand. After years of waiting, not always patiently, the couple was finally given a healthy baby boy fittingly named Isaac, which means "son of laughter." Abraham faithfully placed his trust and expectations on the Lord, and he was not disappointed! Yet when Isaac was still only a boy, God asked Abraham to do the unthinkable: sacrifice his only son.

Why would God ask this of Abraham? Why make him wait a century for his first child and then ask him to kill that child? I'm certain Abraham was asking the same thing. But rather than doubt, Abraham gathered his son, a knife, and wood for the fire, and then he started up the mountain.

> Abraham took the wood for the burnt offering and placed it on his son Isaac, and he himself carried the fire and the knife. As the two of them went on together, Isaac spoke up and said to his father Abraham, 'Father?'

> 'Yes, my son?' Abraham replied. 'The fire and wood are here,' Isaac said, 'but where is the lamb for the burnt offering?' Abraham answered, 'God himself will provide the lamb for the burnt offering, my son.' And the two of them went on together. When they reached the place God had told him about, Abraham built an altar there and arranged the wood on it. He bound his son Isaac and laid him on the altar, on top of the wood. Then he reached out his hand and took the knife to slay his son. But the angel of the Lord called out to him from heaven, 'Abraham! Abraham!' 'Here I am,' he replied. 'Do not lay a hand on the boy,' he said. 'Do not do anything to him. Now I know that you fear God, because you have not withheld from me your son, your only son.' Abraham looked up and there in a thicket he saw a ram caught by its horns. He went over and took the ram and sacrificed it as a burnt offering instead of his son.

> Genesis 22:6–13

As Abraham took Isaac up Mount Moriah to sacrifice him to the Lord, he did not know when the lamb would show up. Abraham simply trusted that the Lord would provide—and He did. Our provider, Jehova Jairo, sees exactly what we need and when we need it. As Abraham and Isaac made their way, God knew when to start the ram up the other side so that it would be in just the right place at just the right time.

How often do I find myself frustrated at the events in my life, not realizing that the ram is just over the hill?

> "So Abraham called that place THE LORD WILL PROVIDE. And to this day it is said, 'On the mountain of the Lord it will be provided.'"
> *Genesis 22:14*

My own story points to Jehova Jairo, the God who provides. When my plans seem to fall apart, He shows up when and where I least expect Him. I had a breakup that gave me the courage to move to Arizona and into a job that refined my skills and honed my passions. I was planning to move to Uganda, Africa, but God used the rejection letter to prepare my heart for a different journey. When I watched my boss step out in faith, he gave me the courage to do something similar. I turned down the job opportunity in Texas and remained in the desert obediently. I painfully watched many of the reasons for staying in Arizona disappear, but in time, I entered the most exciting adventure of my life.

The ram is just around the corner. He provides exactly what we need, exactly when we need it. It may not always be what you expect, but it will always be His best. Trust that when He calls us to sacrifice, the ultimate reward is a deeper intimacy with Him—the author and perfecter.

Do You Trust Him?

What about you? Do you trust that the one who formed you will give you good things? Do you believe 1 Corinthians 2:9, which states, "No eye has seen, no ear has heard, and no mind has imagined what God has prepared for those who love Him"?

The idea behind the bucket-list exercise isn't to stifle your dreams! God loves to hear our heart's desires, to watch us live for more than comfort, and to make goals and achieve them. Goals are good. They are a great way to remain motivated and forward thinking. Goals keep me away from the television and out accomplishing.

Dreams require more than just an errand or a little extra effort. My dreams are the things I whisper in prayer, share carefully, and cultivate in the back of my mind. In order to make my dream list, the item must require more than what I have within *me* to achieve it. Those hopes need a higher power to step in and intervene. Dreams, at least for me, tend to motivate my everyday thinking and living. They keep me living wide-awake and looking for opportunity.

I would encourage you to think about your own list of goals and dreams. Keep adding, keep the list handy, and dream bigger than what you could ask for or imagine. The satisfaction of crossing off completed missions is enjoyable, but it's the process and the journey that makes for the actual living. Just don't forget to ask the chef what He recommends.

So what now?

Take a moment to turn back to your bucket list and consider writing, "I will take whatever you choose to give me. I trust you, Lord." Offer your life and your dreams to your Father. Pray, "God, I trust that You are going to give me a life beyond my wildest dreams. Even though the unknown can be scary, I know that You are for me and You will see me through in this life and into the next. In Jesus' name, amen."

We have a God who says in Matthew 7:11 that He loves to give us just what we need! "If you, then, though you are evil, know how to give good gifts to your children, how much more will your Father in heaven give good gifts to those who ask him!"

Paul reminds us in Philippians 3:8 that everything is a loss compared to knowing Christ. "What is more, I consider everything a loss compared to the surpassing greatness of knowing Christ Jesus my Lord, for whose sake I have lost all things. I consider them rubbish, that I may gain Christ."

As much as I want my list, ultimately I must trust in the one who is the expert on what I need, the one who gives good things and will assure I live the life for which I was created.

> "You will keep in perfect peace him whose mind is
> steadfast, because he trusts in you. Trust in the LORD
> forever, for the LORD, the LORD, is the Rock eternal."
> *Isaiah 26:3–4*

---

*Are you willing to embrace God's plans for
your life, even if they look different from what
you've always pictured? Why or why not?*

My Journal Entry

June 19, 2003

Papa God,

So the question is this: do I actually ever learn something just once and then apply it to my life, or will I be forced to continue to relearn everything over and over until I die? How many times have I read about and prayed about security and contentment? How many times have I been distracted? I know You love me, Lord, and I am ashamed when I need any other love besides You. Love? Attention? Friendship? They all pale in comparison to You. Lord, I prayed for focus, and others are praying for my focus. Please help me. Show me what to do. I am scared of the response. Scared of the best?

Love,
Ginger

Ginger,

Trust my love! No good thing will I withhold from you! You have been asking for the best, and now you want to settle for your better timing? Make up your mind. Meditate on My words and ask for help. I'm here. Are you willing to listen? I love you, and I have the best for you. Wait for me alone!

Love,
God

Your Journal Entry

CHAPTER 7

No Shrinking Back

I have told you these things, so that in me you may have peace. In this world you will have trouble. But take heart! I have overcome the world.
John 16:33

Dear Twenty-Six-Year-Old Ginger,

You know how you always talk about living real life rather than the sham this world offers? Do you remember the thousands of young people you have challenged to wake up and start dreaming and living and creating? It's time for you to listen. You have a desire and a capacity to create and do. This resides in you because you are made in the image of the creator.

It is time to forget fear. It is time to stop making excuses. It is time to make a choice and just go.

Love,
Today's Ginger

Get Out of the Car

"We have to be braver than we think we can be, because God is
constantly calling us to be more than we are, to see through plastic
sham to living, breathing reality, and to break down our defenses
of self-protection in order to be free to receive and give love."
Madeleine L'Engle, Walking on Water[16]

Moving to a new city in your twenties is kind of like starting freshman
year at a public school after having attended the same private school
for the first nine years of your education. You don't know which table
you can sit at, you don't know where your classes are, and you don't
want to look like a nerd, so you memorize the map of the school and
then can't get in on the first day because you didn't want to bring your
schedule (you memorized that, too). And that wouldn't be a problem
except for the fact that only the kids who "don't care" are standing
in line outside the school while waiting for new schedules. They look
like they have knives in their backpacks and want to stab you and your
new first-day-of-school outfit.

I really don't enjoy being in a situation where I do not know a majority
of the company present. When I first moved to Arizona, I was
constantly forcing myself to get out of the car and walk into my own
personal version of torture. Okay, maybe *torture* is too strong of a term.
It was like going to the dentist. That's it. Walking into new situations
and having to feel them out is like going to the dentist: slightly painful
and not overly enjoyable until the very last few minutes.

The thing is, in these situations, I know that I will be fine eventually.
No one (hopefully) is going to be mean to me, hurt me, or put me in
harm's way. At best, I'll have some new friends, and at worst, I will
be completely ignored for an hour or so. Even this knowledge doesn't
make it any easier for me to actually get out of the car, because I'm
really good at arguing with myself.

Often, the discussion goes a little something like this:

Ginger 1: You need to get out of the car and go into this Bible study.

Ginger 2: But I don't know anyone in there.

Ginger 1: That's *why* you are going. So you can make some friends.

Ginger 2: But I have friends.

Ginger 1: Um, it doesn't count if they are eighteen hours away.

Ginger 2: I know, but what if these people—

Ginger 1: Stop making excuses.

Ginger 2: You know, I'm probably at the wrong place. I don't see many cars. I should just go.

Ginger 1: Get out of the car.

Ginger 2: Okay! I'm going!

I am a cautious adventurer. I created the title for myself after years of experience. I'm mildly obsessed with the idea of being adventurous. As a kid, I checked out every "Choose Your Own Adventure" book and spent hours leading my Barbies along the Oregon Trail (which was actually located behind the azalea bushes) to their homes on the coast. As I grew older, I made it my mission to plan trips, collect maps, and record quotes about adventure. I wanted to be the heroine of every story.

There's only one problem: I don't take action. Usually, I sit and I wait, reassuring myself that certainly I have done enough, when actually God is calling me farther out and deeper still. I have learned to be afraid. I fear meeting new people, rejection, cafeteria food, having my heart broken, and long meetings. I fear that if I take a step of faith, it won't actually lead anywhere and I will end up looking foolish. I could go to great lengths to never put myself in a situation where I would have to be afraid, but I would also miss out on a lot of things that this world and our Father have to offer. I could be the safest, most boring person to ever have lived on this earth. But often, the momentous events of my life have come out of situations that were the scariest.

We talked about "risking big in order to win big" in the fifth chapter. That principle can just as easily apply to my daily life as it can to my relationships. There's a man in the Bible who I believe demonstrates this kind of reckless, full-hearted determination. While he didn't always succeed in every challenge, he's the kind of guy who wasn't going down without a fight. The disciple Peter had no problem getting out of the car. Peter would have leapt out of the car while it was still running. (Side note: if you must get out of your car while it's still running, be sure to leave it in park. Not that I've ever done that ...)

Peter was always raring to go, and the results of that passion often had interesting results. One story in particular comes to mind.

Jesus had been ministering all day long. This was the day he fed five thousand people with five loaves of bread and two fish. On top of that, he had just received word that his cousin, John the Baptist, had recently been beheaded. Desiring some time to "go and get some rest" (Mark 6:31), Jesus heads off to a mountainside and sends his disciples across the lake in a boat. You can find the whole story in Matthew 14 starting in verse 25, but I'll give you the abbreviated version.

Jesus crosses the lake sometime between three and six o'clock in the morning. Remember there is no electricity, so it is probably pretty

119

dark. As the disciples look across the lake, they see a figure walking toward them on the water. Of course, they don't realize that it's Jesus. The disciples are afraid that they see a ghost, so they cry out in fear. *Immediately* Jesus tells them to take courage. He tells them not to be afraid, that it's Him, you know, walking on water.

In this moment, Peter chooses to make a special request. "Lord, if it is You, command me to come to you on the water." Odd request, don't you think? I might have gone with, "Lord, if it is You, tell me what we ate for breakfast yesterday." But no, not Peter. Peter says the first thing that comes into his head. And Jesus replies, "Come." How do you like them apples, Peter?

This is the moment when I would have started panicking. "Shoot! Why did I say that?" Who knows what Peter was actually thinking? Matthew doesn't record Peter's words, if he had any. What we do know is that Peter then got out of the boat and walked on the water toward Jesus.

I have no doubt that Peter had a few fearful thoughts in the moment when he put his first leg over the lip of the boat. Did he coach himself over? Did he take a few minutes to set his other foot on the water? Did he stand up slowly, testing the strength of the liquid below him? We don't know. But regardless of what it looked like, he reminds us that stepping out *even while being afraid* is possible. So what if people see our knees shake or hear us scream as we take a step of faith?

2 Timothy 1:7 reads, "For God did not give us a spirit of timidity, but a spirit of power, of love, and of self-discipline." We were not meant to have the word *timid* associated with our faith experience!

Peter *did* something while the other eleven disciples just watched. Peter decided to actually live in the miracle. It was risky, but Peter chose to act rather than just observe. I know from experience that it can be easy for us to allow fear to keep us from experiencing the life that Jesus has for us!

"If you are who you say you are, then tell me to come."

As I seek to live courageously, Peter's story reminds me that the answer to fear is faith. *The answer to fear is faith.*

Sinking

Peter takes his first steps and is actually walking on water. He's so close to Jesus. He is living a miracle, yet he allows fear to creep in when he sees the wind and the waves. "But when he saw the wind, he was afraid and, beginning to sink, cried out, 'Lord, save me!'" (Matthew 14:30).

Sinking. Failure. I read the words of Jesus and add the disappointment I feel toward Peter. Jesus says, "You of little faith, why did you doubt?" (Matthew 14:31).

The perfectionist inside of me wants to shout at the sinking Peter, "Come on! You were walking on water, living a miracle. You were taking the steps I'm too afraid to take, and now you're sinking? Pull it together!"

But I also feel for Peter in that moment. He was so close to Jesus, yet he started to sink. I think I initially read the words of Jesus in an angry tone here, because that's how I perceive His response to me when *I* fail. To be honest, I sometimes view God as an angry parent or teacher just expecting me to mess up again. *"Oh, Ginger, you of little faith."*

But what parent yells at a baby learning to walk? When my friend's baby girl was almost one, she was just starting to walk. Carey invited us all over to her house so that we could watch her little girl take those first few steps. Babies are so funny when they learn to walk. They wobble, hold one leg in the air for what seems like forever, and reach their hands out like someone grasping for the wall in the deep end of a pool. So this beautiful baby girl takes two steps in front of us, and then she just fell. She couldn't even walk! The baby fell. Carey walked over to give her daughter a pep talk and tried to impress upon her the severity of the situation. "Um, baby girl? All these people are here to watch you and you are crumbling. We've worked on this for weeks! Get up. Come on! Get up!"

Okay. You got me. None of that really happened, but Carey's little one *did* learn how to walk and her parents were just about as proud as can be. What do parents usually do when a baby learns to walk? Even if a baby takes just one step and falls, the parents are still ready to pronounce the child an Olympian! They are so excited to watch their child try to walk. If their beloved child falls, they pick him up and set him on his way again.

When Peter begins sinking, Jesus does not count to ten and let him think about what he has done. He doesn't point and laugh. Instead, we read that Jesus *immediately* stretched out His hand and took hold of him. Jesus said, *"Oh, you of little faith, why did you doubt?"*

The phrase "of little faith" is spoken by the Lord only to believers as a *gentle* rebuke for anxiety in the New Testament. It isn't the same rebuke used when Jesus interacts with the Pharisees. When Jesus takes hold of Peter, the wording utilized here actually means "to seize; to catch; to take by the hand, in order to succor; *to heal.*"[17]

Jesus gently reminds Peter, "I'm here, just like I was when you got out of the boat. What happened?"

God is calling to each of us, coaching us through our fears. "Take another step! I will be there if you fail." What risks hold us back from even getting out of the boat?

Peter was the only one of the eleven who could list "walking on water" on his résumé. He took a chance, pushed through his panic, and got out of the boat. He may have felt like a failure, but at least he took a step!

Countless spiritual giants of the Bible took steps in spite of fear, in spite of life-threatening risks.

Moses had to face the enemy (Exodus 7–12).

Esther looked death in the face (Esther 4–5).

Gideon had an army of three hundred with no weapons to face an army of several thousand (Judges 7).

Ezekiel lay on his side by a pile of dung for months (Ezekiel 4).

Isaiah ran naked and barefoot for three years through the city (Isaiah 20).

Hosea was encouraged to marry an unfaithful prostitute (Hosea 1).

Abraham was asked to sacrifice his son (Genesis 22).

Mary was told she would need a maternity-sized wedding dress (Luke 1).

God is big enough for us to voice our fears and proceed even if we are scared, nervous, or anxious. But it is also worthwhile knowing that the most frequent command in Scripture is *do not fear.*

No Fear

In my mind, I'm an adventurer. By nature, I am a creature of habit. I hang my keys in the same place each time I return home. I keep my socks folded and tucked away in their proper drawer. I think that's why I resort to drastic measures when it comes to food selections. When shopping for cereal, I make it my goal to never purchase the same product twice in a row. I could go eight months in-between boxes of Cheerios, one of my favorites. If I don't live on the edge in the morning, I probably won't during the rest of my day. I used to be so predictable that you could guess what I was going to order at any given restaurant. In recent years, I have made it my goal to live life on the edge when dining, to take a risk, and to order the special. If I don't like lunch, I can always eat dinner, right? (Often it's the small victories that make your day.)

I'm not suggesting that food is a major fear for me. It's not. (Quite the opposite, my friends.) I am telling you that my natural tendency is to play it safe. Sometimes, it takes practicing courage in the simpler tasks to remind me that living without fear is possible.

Dictionary.com defines courage as "the quality of mind or spirit that enables a person to face difficulty, danger, pain, etc., without fear; bravery."[18] I love that!

The only problem I have with this definition is that I don't think courage is one of my defining characteristics. The sad truth is that even though I line my bookshelves with inspiration, make life-mission statements that would rival the greatest explorer, and take notes on anything that has to do with adventure, sometimes I'm too afraid to actually explore.

Some time ago, I spoke on the phone with a friend who was contemplating applying for a master's program she feared might be too challenging for her. I started wondering how often we make decisions based on what we are afraid to do. I'm not referring to overcommitting ourselves; sometimes we must say, "No," to things in order to say, "Yes," to what is really important. But when we have the opportunity to take a risk and try, how often do we dismiss the thought because we don't feel we are up to the challenge or the idea frightens us?

I went skiing in northern Arizona where there is, in fact, snow. The high was sixty-eight degrees in Phoenix, but there was plenty of snow in Flagstaff. We pulled out around 5:30 a.m. in order to hit the slopes and make the most of the day. I had not skied in almost a decade, and prior to that, I had skied only sporadically through high school and college. Although I had managed to make it down some runs without breaking a bone or being carried off the mountain on a stretcher, I would not consider myself an expert by any means.

When I took to the slopes this time, I was skiing with a family who was pretty much raised with ski poles in their hands. I was nervous to pick up speed and trying feverishly to keep up with a teenage boy and his mother. I took two runs, doing pretty well, before we jumped on a new lift. I was thankful to have a moment to take in my surroundings and enjoy the experience, but halfway up the lift, my courageous teen friend turned to me and mentioned that this might not be the correct lift for the run we were intending to take.

He was correct. When we reached the top, I discovered the only way down was a death-defying black diamond slope. Inside, I was panicking. This was not part of the plan. Not only was I going to break every bone in my body, but surely I would also lose every piece of personal dignity I had worked so diligently to preserve that day. My friends tried to encourage me by letting me know we would stay clear of moguls, but that didn't really help me in that moment.

I was doing fine for about the first five minutes, and then we came to the steepest portion of the run. My immediate thought was, *No way. No way. I'm not doing this.*

As my two skiing companions headed down, I had a discussion with myself that seemed to go on forever but probably lasted less than five seconds. I had two choices: take off my skis and walk back to the lift or head down the mountain (quite possibly to my death). I made the decision right then that I would never let fear alone be a reason for not experiencing something in life. I will let common sense be a factor, but not fear. I bent my knees, hugged the mountain, and kept my snowplow at the ready.

I was fine, and the feeling at the bottom of the mountain was amazing. I didn't fall, I didn't injure myself, and I had accomplished something that I had initially been terrified to do.

When I talked to my friend who was considering the master's program again, I encouraged her to think all the way through her feelings about the opportunity. It would be one thing for her to decline if she really wasn't interested in it or thought it didn't line up with the course her life was taking. But to say, "No," because of fear of failure—I couldn't let her get away with that. (Even though Ash didn't end up entering the program, she currently lives courageously as a certified nurse on the cardiac floor of a major hospital. She challenges her own fears every day.)

I like to think of courage as more than just doing something we fear. I think courage is taking action despite fear for a purpose. I recognize that there isn't anything amazing in choosing Special K over Cheerios. I don't expect to wake up tomorrow ready to take on the world, but I am taking daily steps toward abandoning fear in every aspect of my life.

Peter may not have always had his walk together, but he certainly shows me what it means to live courageously when he walked on water. There are going to be lots of things that scare you in your life: meeting new people, going off to college, losing your job, getting lost in a big city, etc. But in each of those instances, you can either let the fear paralyze you or you can take heart and take courage.

One of my favorite verses in the Bible comes from Hebrews 10:39. It says, "But we are not of those who shrink back and are destroyed, but of those who believe and are saved." It is a reminder for when we become faint of heart and begin to fear. I am a child of the King of Kings who has overcome the world! I can believe that He will make good on His promises and see me through.

I don't know what keeps you captive to fear, but I do know that I have spent my share of time fearing when I should have chosen courage. I still struggle, but I'm slowly learning to process my fears using wisdom and the truth in God's Word to move from fear to faith. I can choose to be ruled by my emotions and fears or I can claim the words of God found in the Bible!

When God promises you something, you can take it to the bank. Over and over, He says to you, "You are valuable. I am for you. I love you. I have work for us to do, and I will be the one to see it to completion."

Will we trust Him?

> "Faith is believing or trusting a person, and its reasonableness
> depends on the reliability of the person being trusted.
> It is always reasonable to trust the trustworthy. And
> there is nobody more trustworthy than God."
> *John Stott, Romans*[19]

I may not know the source of your fears and how big they really are, but I do know how mighty, awesome, powerful, and personal our God is. He will be with you wherever you are and wherever you go.

So what holds you back from total abandon? Make a list of your fears if you want. Write them out in the space provided.

I'm afraid of …

- » Family members dying

- » Cancer

- » Having someone dislike my work

- » Ending up alone

Now I want you to take each of those items and put God's words and promises into the mix. Rewrite the truth in the space provided below. Here's what I mean:

» I'm afraid of one day being diagnosed with cancer, but even if that happens, God is still God and He says that He is the great healer (Luke 4:23).

» If people dislike my creative work, God still "doesn't want us to be shy with His gifts, but bold and loving and sensible" (Timothy 1:7 MSG).

» If all of my friends have dates or are getting married and I'm alone, "God goes with [me]; he will never leave [me] nor forsake [me]" (Deuteronomy 31:6).

Whatever your fear, the Lord is the answer. Jesus knew that His disciples would have times of fear, which is why He said in John 16:33, "I have told you these things, so that in Me you may have peace. In this world you will have trouble. But take heart! I have overcome the world."

Note that He did not say that they *might* have trouble, but that they *will* have trouble. This is a broken world where death and heartache abound, but that does not mean we are defeated! Jesus promises that the final victory is won and that death has been defeated. He has overcome this world and will redeem it. It is because of that promise that we are *not* those who shrink back but those who place our leg over the side of the boat and step out toward our Savior!

> "What we fear is what we're subject to; our fears define our master. When we fear God and God only, we are no longer bound by all of the other fears that would hold us captive. The fear of death, the fear of failure, the fear of rejection, the fear of insignificance—all ... become powerless when we know the fear of the Lord ... Perfect love casts out all fear."
> *Erwin McManus, The Barbarian Way*[20]

What will it take for you to abandon fear, get out of the car, and live with wonder and faith? You were made an original, so step up and live the life to which you've been called. If you feel as though your relationship with the Lord isn't growing, your life is anything but extraordinary, and your past is eating away at your future, then consider how much fear is ruling your life.

The call that was given to Peter is there for you as well. "Come!" he says to us.

Take heart, take a risk, and take a step. He's there to catch you when you fall, and He will be so proud of you for trying.

"Teach me your way, O LORD, and I will walk in your truth;
give me an undivided heart, that I may fear your name."
Psalm 86:11

---

*Are you letting fear or faith lead the
way in your decision-making?*

My Journal Entry

January 8, 2007

All in all, it was a good day, but 50 percent of it was spent alone. In fact, 50 percent of this week was spent alone. I have got to put myself out there and try to meet people. They aren't just going to knock on my door!

Please let me find a community of people my own age! I am tired of living vicariously through the stories I see on TV. Sometimes, I feel like I'm just watching my own life, waiting for the next exciting thing to be on. I'm playing it safe while I just pay the bills and get my job done. So for now, I want to ditch my TV in favor of real relationships and time well spent.

I ask for courage and resolve, Lord.

Your Journal Entry

CHAPTER 8

For the Good

My flesh and my heart may fail, but God is the
strength of my heart and my portion forever.
Psalm 73:26

Dear Ginger—at every phase of your life,

Stop comparing your story to the stories of other women. Stop comparing your life to theirs. Trust the one who loves you best to give you His best in His time.

Love,
Today's Ginger

His Good

"I do know that waiting on God requires the willingness to bear uncertainty, to carry within oneself the unanswered question, lifting the heart to God about it whenever it intrudes upon one's thoughts."
Elizabeth Elliot, Passion and Purity[21]

When I left everything familiar in Texas and moved to Arizona as a determined twenty-five year-old, I was certain that the key lesson was going to be independence. I was sorely mistaken. This road has led me to deep places of *dependence*. I've learned some amazing things from my years of singleness. For me, marriage and relationships became an idol that I knew, if given too many of my thoughts, would lead to heartache. It was the ultimate desire of my heart for a long time. I wanted a homecoming date, a prom date, and a boyfriend. I wanted someone celebrating with me and cheering me on. I wanted the cards, flowers, New Year's kiss, and Valentine's Day date. There were so many years when I didn't trust God. I didn't want Him to help. I didn't believe that His dreams could be better than mine. It's awful to type it out, but I began to hide my deepest desires and hopes from God. I was crying out, "God, I need someone! I want someone! Everyone else has someone. This is my desire, so why aren't You giving me this?"

I questioned God's timing and withholding, and I am certain that I felt His response deep in my heart. "Ginger, do you think I love you less because your life doesn't look exactly the way you dreamed it would?"

Singleness was not my cross to bear. Singleness was not and is not a condition that is waiting for a cure. My story taught me resolve and how to set my expectations on God. This time of wrestling brought me to a deeper and richer relationship with the Lord.

Even today, I am guilty of doubting that God's promises are good. That is so sad and so disheartening to say, but the way that I spend time worrying or fearing proves that fact. I don't always trust that His good is going to really be good. In my mind, my good is the best that I can think and dream up.

We serve a God who loves to give good gifts in His perfect timing. He wants to hear from us and know the desires of our hearts. We don't have to be ashamed of our requests or fearful of His response. He is not stingy, tired, or busy. In fact, His promise is that I cannot comprehend all that He desires to give me!

> "No eye has seen, no ear has heard, no mind has conceived
> what God has prepared for those who love him."
> *1 Corinthians 2:9*

God is God. He knows what I need, and I must trust Him to carry out the good work He started in me until completion. God has given us work to do, and He promises in the midst of this crazy, broken world that He will bring things together for the good. "And we know that in all things God works *for the good* of those who love Him, who have been called according to His purpose. For those God foreknew He also predestined to be conformed to the likeness of His Son" (Romans 8:28–29, emphasis added).

I think we often read this verse and interpret it to mean God makes everything easy. Or God makes everything perfect like butterflies, rainbows, and mocha lattes. Ninety-eight percent of the time, I desire comfort, safety, and ease more than anything else—at times even more than God. Comfort (and not just the kind that involves good food and a soft bed) can quickly become my idol. I like feeling safe, cared for, and worry free. Let's shut down conflict, stay in the air-conditioning, volunteer when it's convenient, give when asked, sleep when we're tired, purchase when and what we want to, and above all else, let's take it easy.

We don't associate *good* with pain.

Did God love His son Jesus? Did God allow Jesus to experience pain? Yes and yes.

"And we know that in all things God works for the good of those who love Him ..."

My life certainly hasn't always been filled with good things. I've failed tests, been sick, lost friends and family members, struggled with an eating disorder and experienced breakups and disappointments. None of those are filed under "Good Times for Ginger."

"And we know that in all things God works for the good of those who love Him, who have been called according to His purpose. For those God foreknew He also predestined to be conformed to the likeness of His Son ..."

What does it mean to conform to something? Have you ever used a Jell-O mold? You put some green liquid into a shape, wait for a few hours while it chills in the fridge, and then voila! Jell-O teddy bear. The liquid has conformed.

Romans 8:29 shows us that God's desire, His best, what He deems to be good, is that we be conformed to the likeness of His son. The Message version says God's good is designed to "shape the lives of those who love Him along the same lines as the life of His Son."

I use good to mean a lot of things. "How was the movie?" "So good!" "You want seconds?" "No thanks, I'm good." "Are you too hot?" "Nah, I'm good." How was school?" "Good."

God's love redefines *good.*

Good does not guarantee comfort, ease, or safety. Good sometimes means going *through* the fire rather than *around* it.

My role here on this earth is to glorify God with my life. The closer I draw to the Father, the more I will begin to look like His son. That's *true* beauty. Being beautiful is living out the unique calling God has placed on your life.

God loves me enough to take me to the places I don't always want to go, to work on my heart until it is His. Our hearts are quick to doubt, prone to wander, and downright selfish, but placed in the right hands, our hearts are things of beauty. They can expand to welcome the hurting. They can break with compassion for the orphan. They can mend even after having been repeatedly crushed. Our hearts are worth sharing and valuable enough to protect.

Yet 1 John 3:20 says, "God is greater than our hearts and He knows everything."

God knows everything. So where was God in my heartaches? Right alongside me, like He always is. God's grace is sufficient for me; His power is made perfect in my weakness. He knows the days that I vocalize worries and fears in my journal. He has read every word. He sees my tears, and He is greater than the worries in my heart. He knows what I really want. More than that, He knows how to bring out His good in my life.

Honestly, it is hard to trust when you are in the mist of the in-between stages of life and you feel like everyone else is a step ahead. But just because something is difficult, doesn't mean it isn't worthwhile. Trust that His good *is* good. Even if your life does not look like anything *you* had planned for it, remember that our Father loves to give you the desires of your heart. Not every desire will come to fruition in your timing or in the way you might have expected. But the promise of God assures us that He is enough to *satisfy* every single longing. He has not forgotten you. He has not forsaken you. He is pleased with you because He is pleased with His son; He cannot love you any more or any less than He does right now.

If we really believed God loved us, it would change everything.

> We would recognize our value and identity come from Him alone.

> We could stop comparing ourselves with others.

> Praise and criticism wouldn't make or break our days.

> We would readily guard and share our hearts.

> We would move from guilt over past relationship mistakes to freedom in forgiveness.

> Our joy and happiness would not be dependent upon others, especially guys.

> Our expectations, hopes, and dreams would rest securely in Him.

> We would have the courage to confidently follow wherever He calls.

Won't you give your heart to the one who formed you in the depths of the earth? Turn over to Him your fears, your doubts, and your mistakes. He is gentle enough to hold you while strong enough to bind up your bleeding wounds. I know this from experience. "The

LORD is close to the brokenhearted and saves those who are crushed in spirit" (Psalm 34:18).

My Savior has captured my heart, and He has won my love. I still have days when I do not trust, when I worry, and when I doubt. But He is right where He has always been, waiting for me to seek Him with all of my heart.

> "Hear, O Israel: The LORD our God, the LORD is one. Love the LORD your God with all your heart and with all your soul and with all your strength. These commandments that I give you today are to be upon your hearts."
> *Deuteronomy 6:4–6*

Do you believe that His good really is good?

My Journal Entry

November 1, 2009

Lord, I want *You* first. I want Your dreams. I want the life You have for me—Your plans, Your goals. I would give up any of mine to be able to hear from You and see what You desire. If that includes having someone by my side, fighting the fight together, I'm in. But more than that, I just want You, Lord. I trust You. Let my heartbeat match Yours.

Thank you for this time of rich abundance. I cannot believe how far You have brought me. You have blessed me beyond measure. In the midst of so many empty blanks in my future, I am amazed. Thank You for the path—the lessons, the tears, and even the disappointments. Thank You for the story you are writing with my life.

Thank You that Your good is so, so good.

"Praise our God, O peoples, let the sound of his praise be heard; he has preserved our lives and kept our feet from slipping. For you, O God, tested us; you refined us like silver. You brought us into prison and laid burdens on our backs. You let men ride over our heads; we went through fire and water, but you brought us to a place of abundance."
Psalm 66:8–12

Your Journal Entry

"Be at rest once more, O my soul, for the
Lord has been good to you."
Psalm 116:7

O Love that wilt not let me go,
I rest my weary soul in thee;
I give thee back the life I owe,
That in Thine ocean depths its flow
May richer, fuller be.

O joy that seekest me through pain,
I cannot close my heart to thee;
I trace the rainbow through the rain,
And feel the promise is not vain
That morn shall tearless be.

George Matheson[22]

About the Author

Texas-born GINGER CIMINELLO is a passionate writer and speaker who communicates through storytelling and dramatic narrative. Her awkward middle-school phase lasted almost ten years, allowing her to connect with students in a humorous and personal way. Ginger holds a deep desire to reach her audiences and encourage them to laugh, learn from her mistakes, and look up to the heavenly Father. Her own story contains embarrassing moments, a two-year bout with an eating disorder, being abandoned at the prom, and finally finding contentment in knowing who God has made her to be.

Ginger holds a bachelor's degree in theater ministry from Abilene Christian University and has over ten years of speaking experience at churches, camps, and educational groups. She worked for six years in camping ministry with Pine Cove Christian Camps in Tyler, Texas, before making her way to the desert of Arizona. Ginger currently lives in Phoenix with her eHarmony-matched husband, David, and their daughter.

Ginger writes a weekly blog to continue the conversations that start every time she walks into an auditorium, classroom, or sanctuary. Come and join the conversation.

gingerciminello.com
twitter.com/gingercim
facebook.com/gingercim

Endnotes

1. Strong, James. *Strong's Exhaustive Concordance of the Bible. Entry 7965.* Hendrickson, 2007.

2. "Self-esteem." Dictionary.com. Random House Dictionary. 2013. http://dictionary.reference.com/browse/self-esteem (22 May 2013).

3. Montgomery, L. M. *Anne of Green Gables* (New York City: Bantam Classic; Later Printings edition, 1987).

4. Shakespeare, William. *Hamlet* (The New Folger Library Shakespeare). Simon & Schuster; New Folger Edition, 2003.

5. DiMarco, Hayley. "You Cannot Seek Anyone with All Your Heart in Your Spare Time." June 14, 2011 (Tweet).

6. Batterson, Mark. *In a Pit with a Lion on a Snowy Day* (Colorado Springs: Multnomah, 2006), 30.

7. Moore, Beth. *Praying God's Word* (Nashville: Broadman & Holman, 2000), 3.

8. Moore, Beth. *Living Beyond Yourself: Exploring the Fruit of the Spirit - Video Sessions.* Week 2, Video Session 1. (Nashville: LifeWay Christian Resources, 2004).

9. "Entrust." TheFreeDictionary.com. The American Heritage® Dictionary of the English Language, Fourth Edition copyright ©2000 by Houghton Mifflin Company. http://www.thefreedictionary.com/entrust (May 29, 2013).

10. Connally, Gilliam. *Revelations of a Single Woman* (Carol Stream: Tyndale House, 2006), 12.

11. *The Princess Bride,* Dir. Rob Reiner. Perf. Mandy Patinkin. 1987.

12. Dake, Finis Jennings. *Dake's Annotated Reference Bible* (Lawrenceville: Dake Bible Sales, 1991), 643.

13. "How to Prevent Teenagers from Sexting and Protect Them from Other Teens Who Do." Reputation.com. N.p., n.d. Web. May 28, 2013.

14. Lewis, C. S. *The Four Loves* (New York: Harcourt Brace Jovanovich, 1960), 169.

15. DiMarco, Hayley and Michael. *The Art of Rejection* (Grand Rapids: Fleming H. Revell, 2006), 105–106.

16. L'Engle, Madeleine. *Walking on Water* (New York: North Point Press, 1995), 67.

17. *The Hebrew-Greek Key Word Study Bible.* New Testament Dictionary entry, 1949. AMG Publishers, 2008.

18. "Courage." Dictionary.com. Random House Dictionary. 2013. http://dictionary.reference.com/browse/courage (28 May 2013).

19. Stott, John R. W. *Romans: God's Good News for the World* (Downers Grove: InterVarsity Press, 1994), 133.

20. McManus, Erwin. *The Barbarian Way* (Nashville: Thomas Nelson, 2005), 101-102.

21. Elliot, Elisabeth. *Passion and Purity* (Grand Rapids: Fleming H. Revell, 1984), 59-60.

22. Matheson, George. *"O Love That Will Not Let Me Go."* Church of Scotland magazine *Life and Work*, January 1882.

CPSIA information can be obtained at www.ICGtesting.com
Printed in the USA
LVOW06s0702010913

350475LV00002B/4/P